THE FOUNTAINWELL DRAMA TEXTS

General Editors
T. A. DUNN
ANDREW GURR
JOHN HORDEN
A. NORMAN JEFFARES
R. L. C. LORIMER

Assistant General Editor
BRIAN W. M. SCOBIE

8

THOMAS MIDDLETON

A TRICK TO CATCH THE OLD ONE

Edited by
CHARLES BARBER

UNIVERSITY OF CALIFORNIA PRESS
Berkeley and Los Angeles · 1968

University of California Press
Berkeley and Los Angeles, California

First Published   1968

Library of Congress Catalog Card No.: 68-64526

Originally published by Oliver and Boyd Ltd,
Edinburgh, Scotland

© 1968—Critical Introduction, Note on the Text, Text as printed, Textual Notes, Commentary, Bibliography, Glossary, and Appendix—Charles Barber.

Printed in Great Britain

PREFACE

The first bibliographical analysis of the early editions of the play: George R. Price's "The Early Editions of *A Trick to catch the old one*", in *The Library*, Fifth series, XXII 3, pp. 205–27 appeared in September 1967 when this edition was already in proof. At that late stage I was unable to make as much use of Professor Price's findings as I should have liked, but I have managed to incorporate some of them, mainly in footnotes to my *Note on the Text*. To facilitate this late insertion of material, I regularly cite the article simply as "Early Editions".

Dr Andrew Gurr has acted as General Textual Editor for this play, and I should like to express my warm gratitude for the help which he has so generously given me, despite the heavy pressure of other work. Such ability as I have been able to acquire as a textual editor I have learnt from him.

I should also like to offer my thanks, for their unfailing courtesy and helpfulness, to the Librarians and library-staffs of the British Museum, the Bodleian Library, the Victoria and Albert Museum, Trinity College Cambridge, Eton College, and the University of Leeds.

CHARLES BARBER

Leeds
November 1967

CONTENTS

CRITICAL INTRODUCTION	1
A NOTE ON THE TEXT	9
A TRICK TO CATCH THE OLD ONE	15
TEXTUAL NOTES	83
COMMENTARY	89
BIBLIOGRAPHY	99
GLOSSARY	101
APPENDIX	107

CRITICAL INTRODUCTION

We know from the title-page that *A Trick to Catch the Old One* was performed by the Children of Paul's, who probably stopped acting in the middle of 1606. It is hardly likely to have been written before 1604, for it is one of the most accomplished of Middleton's early comedies; and if Sampson is right in his explanation of "Poovyes new buildings",[1] it cannot have been written before 1605. So the most probable date is 1605–6.[2] There is no obvious literary source for the incidents in the play. Like Middleton's other early comedies, it probably draws on jest-books, rogue-pamphlets, contemporary gossip and anecdote (London was a small place), and on real people and events, though all these are modified by the dramatic tradition, with its stock situations and characters.[3] The central device of the plot, the passing-off of a woman as a wealthy widow, is found in several plays written between 1605 and 1610; it had probably become common property in anecdote and literary tradition.[4] It has been suggested that Middleton's play owes something to the *Persa* of Plautus;[5] but the resemblances are superficial and the differences great, and I do not think that any influence can be demonstrated.

A Trick to Catch the Old One was one of a number of comedies that Middleton wrote early in his career for the Children of Paul's. It was written, therefore, for the élite audience which had grown up in the private theatres since the re-appearance of the boys' companies at the turn of the century. As yet there was no absolute cleavage between public-theatre and private-theatre drama: it was possible, for example,

---

[1] See Commentary, III. IV. 4.
[2] On the general chronology of Middleton's works, see R. H. Barker. *Thomas Middleton*. New York and London (Columbia U.P., Oxford U.P.) 1958.
[3] See R. C. Bald, "The Sources of Middleton's City Comedies", in *J.E.G.P.*, XXXIII (1934), pp. 373–87; M. G. Christian, "Middleton's Acquaintance with the *Merrie Conceited Jests of George Peele*", in *P.M.L.A.*, L (1935), pp. 753–60; M. Fisher, "Notes on the Sources of some Incidents in Middleton's London Plays", in *R.E.S.*, XV (1939), pp. 283–93.
[4] S. Falk, "Plautus' *Persa* and Middleton's *A Trick to Catch the Old One*", in *M.L.N.*, LXVI (1951), pp. 19–21.
[5] S. Falk, *op. cit.*

for a play written for one type of theatre to be later performed at the other type; but the private theatres did cater for a distinctive taste.[6] This taste was anti-romantic, inclining towards the satirical, the realistic, and the witty. It liked neatness, and admired the single plot rather than the multiple plots of the public theatre. Our play has a single plot (if we neglect the strange scenes with Dampit), and it is handled in a masterly way. Everything arises out of the original impersonation, and situation after situation is developed from it, the whole thing moving with tremendous pace and verve. The story, admittedly, is improbable, which is one reason why the play is sometimes called a farce[7]; but improbability of plot need not prevent a play from being in important senses realistic.

"Realistic", indeed, is one of the words often applied to Middleton's early comedies. By this is usually meant a minute depiction of contemporary habits and manners, a surface verisimilitude, so that we feel that we know Jacobean London better. But *A Trick to Catch the Old One* is realistic in a more important way, in that it presents clearly and unsentimentally some of the social tensions of Jacobean England.[8]

Socially, the play is set on the fluid boundary between citizen and gentleman. Witt-good is of the landed gentry, while his creditors are shopkeeping citizens. In between stand Lucre and Hoord, the New Men of Jacobean England, moneylenders and capitalists; they take the style of gentleman, but are eager to acquire land to put the seal on their status. Lucre is the younger son of a land-owning family who has gone into business. Hoord has citizen origins—his father was "free ath Fishmongers"[9]; the great attraction of the widow is that she will bring him an estate, and he daydreams of the life of a country gentleman.[10]

---

[6] Failure to distinguish different audiences and different theatrical tastes vitiates H. B. Bullock's "Thomas Middleton and the Fashion in Playmaking", in *P.M.L.A.*, XLII (1927), pp. 766–76, which tries to explain Middleton's early comedies as "giving the public what it wanted".

[7] *e.g.* by D. J. Enright, in "Elizabethan and Jacobean Comedy", in *A Guide to English Literature*, 2 *The Age of Shakespeare*, ed. Boris Ford, pp. 416–28. London (Penguin Books) 1955.

[8] For an admirable account of the social background to Jacobean comedy, see L. C. Knights *Drama and Society in the Age of Jonson*. London (Chatto and Windus) 1937. Knights, however, argues that Middleton is not a realist in any important sense.

[9] *A Trick to Catch the Old One* (the present edition hereafter cited as *Trick*), V. II. 21–2.

[10] *Trick*, IV. IV. 50–3.

When he plans the ostentation befitting a member of the landed gentry —a train of liveried servants—his citizen thriftiness asserts itself, and he insists that they shall all be skilled workmen: "I will not keepean idle man about mee."[11] It is a world of social mobility, where, as Lucre says, "most of our beginnings must bee winckt at".[12]

The play deals with the attempt of the bankrupt landed gentleman to get even with the New Men who have fleeced him. The prodigality that has ruined Witt-good is a typical quality of the old-style aristocracy: thrift was not gentlemanly, ostentation was; a gentleman had to live up to his income, or above it.[13] Witt-good's riotous living is the negative side of "housekeeping", the hospitality of the great house, whose passing was so lamented by traditionalists at this period. But when Witt-good addresses himself to outwitting the business-men, he has to resort to sharp practices: to beat them, he has to become like them. In Jacobean England, the play says, the landed gentleman has to adopt the ethics of the New Man if he wishes to survive. All the main characters in the play are rogues. Witt-good recovers his whole estate (not merely the part of it to which Lucre has no real right); he gets his debts paid by Hoord (who has never harmed him); he cheats his creditors, for they are paid less than 13s. 4d in the pound, when in fact he has his estate back and could discharge his debts in full; and he marries off his mistress to Hoord, so that he himself can marry a portion of £1000. He has learnt how to get on in the world.

In the world in which he lives, human relationships are dominated by money; love and marriage are a matter of hard cash. Monylove says "I am to lay out for my fortunes else where",[14] as if a wife were just another investment. Witt-good asks, "will I hugge foure hundred a yeare?"[15] as though he contemplated sexual intercourse with the estate itself. The Curtizan, who loves Witt-good, allows him to marry her off to a rich old man without a word of protest, indeed with gratitude. Marriage is a contract, and is discussed in legal terms. Lucre's wife tells her son to "withdrawe the Action" of his love from the Neece, as

[11] *Trick*, IV. IV. 16.
[12] *Trick*, IV. II. 81f.
[13] See R. Kelso, *The Doctrine of the English Gentleman in the Sixteenth Century*, pp. 81–91. Urbana, Ill. (University of Illinois) 1929.
[14] *Trick*, II. II. 3f.
[15] *Trick*, I. II. 46.

though it were a legal process[16]; the widow is said to have "Nonsuted" many wealthy suitors[17]; and the pun on amorous and legal suitors is frequent. The "romantic" story of Witt-good's marriage to the Neece is treated with the utmost perfunctoriness; and his rapture on the recovery of his estate[18] is much more heartfelt than anything he ever says about the woman he marries.

It is also a competitive world, a jungle of each against each. The creditors combine against Witt-good, but as soon as there is a prospect of profit they try to outsmart one another, each aiming to corner Witt-good for himself. The whole success of Witt-good's trick hinges on the competitiveness of Lucre and Hoord. This began in the economic sphere, but has been carried over into all their relationships. Witt-good plays on it with great skill, and it is this alone that makes the success of his trick plausible.

At the same time, there is a curious kind of innocence about the characters. We do not feel (as we do in Jonson's *Volpone*) that they are utterly perverse and vicious. This is partly because of Middleton's complete lack of obsession with his characters and their vices. His detachment from them is possible because he does not take sides in the social antagonisms depicted in the play: he is not presenting a case for the way of life either of the gentry or of the citizenry. This is one reason, I think, why he is so often compared unfavourably with Jonson and Massinger, in whose best comedies the vices of the New Men are so firmly "placed" morally by reference to traditional standards. It is not self-evident, however, that this taking of sides in a social conflict (which is what Jonson's and Massinger's moral "placing" implies) is an unmixed virtue. In Massinger's comedy *A New Way to Pay Old Debts* (which takes part of its plot from *A Trick to Catch the Old One*, and is usually compared favourably with it[19]), it leads to an idealising of the aristocracy, and to everything being made "nicer" and more genteel than in Middleton (the Curtizan, for example, being replaced by a real rich widow). We are expected to admire Lovel,

---

[16] *Trick*, II. I. 352.
[17] *Trick*, II. I. 89.
[18] *Trick*, IV. II. 91–8.
[19] *e.g.* by A. H. Cruikshank, *Philip Massinger*, pp. 205–8. Oxford (Clarendon Press) 1920; L. C. Knights, *Drama and Society in the Age of Jonson*, p. 274; D. J. Enright, "Elizabethan and Jacobean Comedy", p. 424. A notable exception is M. C. Bradbrook, *The Growth and Structure of Elizabethan Comedy*, p. 157. London (Chatto and Windus) 1955.

a snob who scorns to mix his scarlet blood with the London-blue of Margaret Overreach; and we are expected to believe that the formidable Overreach is defeated by the mediocrities who oppose him. Massinger's picture of the antagonism between New Men and old aristocracy is blurred by his traditionalist stance; Middleton's picture is sharp and astringent.

In Middleton's play there is no retribution. Both Hoord and Lucre overreach themselves, but are not seriously damaged; and Witt-good, the cleverest scoundrel of the lot, gets away with everything. This does not mean that the characters are held up for admiration. Events are consistently seen in an ironic light, and even the conventional moral speeches that end the play undermine themselves by their own knowingness.[20]

Middleton's principal comic technique is dramatic irony: in incident after incident, the audience knows more than the character who is speaking, so that his words take on a significance of which he himself is unaware. So Hoord soliloquises on the joys of marriage and of a landed estate:

> What a Sweet blessing hast thou Maister *Hoord* above a multitude... when I wake I thinke of her lands that revives me, when I go to bed, I dreame of her beauty, and thats ynough for me, she's worth 4. hundred a yeare in her very smock, if a man knewe how to use it, but the journey will bee all in troth into the Country, to ride to her Lands...[21]

This gets its effect by the contrast between Hoord's daydream and our knowledge of the truth; and to the audience the phrase "she's worth 4. hundred a yeare in her very smock" takes on a meaning of which Hoord is innocent, suggesting that Mistress Jane Hoord is a very expensive courtesan.

Sometimes there are characters on the stage who share the audience's knowledge, and help to point up the situation. When the Scrivener reads the release,[22] with its long-winded listing of the widow's property (descending even to dove-houses and rabbit-burrows), this gets its

---

[20] See R. B. Parker, "Middleton's Experiments with Comedy and Judgement", in *Stratford-upon-Avon Studies I, Jacobean Theatre*, ed. J. R. Brown and B. Harris, pp. 179–99. London (Edward Arnold) 1960.
[21] *Trick*, IV. IV. 1–10.
[22] *Trick*, IV. IV. 239–55.

splendid comic effect not only from our knowledge about the widow's true possessions but also from Witt-good's straight-faced acting of his part. Sometimes there are characters on the stage who share the audience's knowledge in varying degrees. Lucre tells the widow how sought-after his nephew is:

> if hee were once knowne to bee in towne, hee would bee presently sought after, nay and happie were they, that could catch him first.[23]

The old fox is speaking the truth (Witt-good would be pursued by his creditors), but thinks that the widow will take only the surface meaning; but the audience knows that the Curtizan knows that Lucre is equivocating, and this gives great expressiveness to her simple reply—"I thinke so?" In the scene at Coldharbour[24] Lucre and Hoord triumph slyly over one another, each thinking that he is a jump ahead (Hoord because he is married to the widow without Lucre knowing it, Lucre because she has come to a secret understanding with him); but the audience is two jumps ahead, knowing that the Curtizan has equivocated with Lucre, but also knowing that Hoord's triumph is a hollow one. Every twist of the plot is exploited in this way with layers of dramatic irony.

Middleton relies much more on this technique than on imagery or richness of language: a phrase in itself commonplace becomes highly charged simply from the situation it is spoken in. The language of the play, all the same, is racy and energetic: the private theatre has not yet lost its rootedness in popular speech. There is often a use of popular proverb: "When the fire growes too unreasonable hotte, ther's no better way then to take of the wood",[25] "set the Hares head to the Goose-giblet".[26] The title of the play is itself proverbial, and of course "the Old-one" suggests the devil.

The characters of the play are type-figures, as can be seen from the kind of names they are given; yet they take on a remarkable psychological verisimilitude. Lucre, for example, identifies himself fully with the roles that he acts, and often goes on acting them even when alone. This is seen when he puts on his new attitude to Witt-good on learning about the widow:

[23] *Trick*, II. I. 315–17.
[24] *Trick*, IV. I.
[25] *Trick*, I. III. 55–6.
[26] *Trick*, IV. IV. 189–90.

Ah Sirrah, that rich widdow, 400. a yeare, beside I here she layes Clayme to a title of a hundred more, this falls unhappily that he should beare a Grudge to me now being likely to prove so rich, what ist tro that hee makes me a Stranger for?[27]

His active imagination has invented the widow's claim to the extra hundred (he has only just heard of her, and she's a fiction anyway); and, while perfectly conscious that he has cheated Witt-good and turned him out of the house, he is already acting the part he is going to put on for his benefit ("what ist tro that hee makes me a Stranger for?"). It is in all seriousness, too, that Lucre reminds Witt-good of the great trouble and expense he has been put to in collecting the rent from Witt-good's estate.[28]

Hoord, on the other hand, combines a sharp business-sense with bonhomie and a tendency to daydream. He is hardly done by in the play, and the audience would feel sorry for him (especially when he turns reproachfully to Witt-good at the end) were it not that after all the Curtizan is too good for him, and he has really made a very lucky marriage.

A remarkably realised character, but one which has no connection with the plot of the play, is Dampit. He is plainly intended as a figure of fun, with his bombastic private language of cant and nonce-words; but in fact he is rather a disturbing figure, with what Parker has called his "incoherent and almost maniac" energy.[29] It has been suggested that he is a take-off of some real person well known to the audience[30]; this is plausible, but he can also be seen as a kind of symbol of the incoherence and rottenness of the usuring society depicted in the play, as he lies "like a noysome dunghill" on his deathbed, scoundrelly to no purpose, and surrounded by unpleasant friends who make smug moral comments and play practical jokes on him.[31]

We know from the 1608 title-page that the play was performed by the Children of Paul's and by the Children of the Blackfriars, and that

[27] *Trick*, II. I. 158–62.
[28] *Trick*, IV. II. 55–6.
[29] R. B. Parker, *op. cit.*, p. 188.
[30] *Thomas Middleton*, ed. M. W. Sampson, p. 17. New York (American Book Co.) 1915.
[31] For an admirable study of Dampit, see R. Levin, "The Dampit Scenes in *A Trick to Catch the Old One*", in *M.L.Q.*, XXV (1964), pp. 140–52.

it had been played before the king. It was still remembered after the Restoration: according to John Downes,[32] it was one of the plays produced by Davenant at the Theatre, Lincoln's Inn Fields, between 1662 and 1665. But after this it seems to have fallen completely out of the repertory of the English theatre. It was revived at the Mermaid Theatre, London, in October 1952; the producer was Joan Swinstead.

[32] *Roscius Anglicanus*, pp. 19–20, 26. London, 1708. This reference is due to Dyce.

A NOTE ON THE TEXT

The following entry appears in the Stationers' Register[1] under the date 7 October 1607:

> George Elde   Entred for his copies vnder th(e) (h)andes of Sir GEORGE BUCK and th(e) wardens. Twoo plaies th(e) one called *the revengers tragedie* th(e) other. *A trick to catche the old one* ... xij^d

Elde published *A Trick to Catch the Old One* in 1608, as a quarto. An examination of the running-titles suggests that two skeleton formes were used. There is no very obvious evidence (*e.g.* from speech-prefixes, spellings) to show how many compositors set it up, and a full-scale compositor analysis (using *e.g.* the evidence of damaged types) is outside the scope of the present edition.[2] The text of the play begins on A3r and ends on H4r. The only prelim is the title-page; this occurs in two forms, which I shall call X and Y.

X reads as follows: A | Trick to catch the | Old-one. | *As it hath beene lately Acted,* | *by the Children of* | *Paules.* | [Printer's device] | AT LONDON | Printed by *George Eld*, and are to be sold at his | house in Fleete-lane at the signe of the | Printers-Presse. | 1608. |.

I have collated one copy with an X title-page, Bodleian Library Malone 797. In this, the title-page is on A2r, while A1 is missing.[3] The collation is A2–4, B–H⁴.

Y reads as follows: A | Tricke to Catch the | Old-one. | As it hath beene often in Action, both | at Paules, and the Black- | Fryers. | *Presented before his Maiestie on* | *New-yeares night last.* | Composde

---

[1] *A Transcript of the Registers of the Company of Stationers of London. 1554–1640 A.D.*, ed. Edward Arber (5 vols.). London, 1875–94.

[2] Price ("Early Editions") finds evidence for two compositors, possibly helped by a third, and thinks that the setting was by formes.

[3] Greg records one other copy with an X title-page, at Harvard; but Price now states that this copy in fact has a Y title-page. The British Museum copy Ashley 1158 has both title-pages, first X and then Y; however, X is not conjugate with anything, while Y is A1 (A2 being cancelled), so the X title-page has probably been taken from another copy; I have therefore counted Ashley 1158 as a Y-type copy.

by T. M. | [Printer's device] | AT LONDON | Printed by *G: E.* and are to be sold by *Henry Rockytt,* | *at the long shop in the Poultrie vnder* | *the Dyall.* 1608. |.

I have collated six copies with a Y title-page: two in the British Museum (C.34.d.42 and Ashley 1158), two in the Victoria and Albert Museum (6554.26. Box 33.1 and 2), one in the Bodleian Library (Malone 812), and one in the library of Eton College.[4] In all these, the title-page is on A1r, and A2 is cancelled.[5] The collation is therefore A1, A3–4, B–H[4].

It is not unusual in this period for an edition to have variant title-pages. In view of the extra information on Y, it is quite likely that X was the original title-page and that the sheets were passed through the press again for the substitution of Y when Rockytt acquired them; but it is not impossible that both title-pages were printed at the original impression, and the sheets shared between Elde and Rockytt. Greg,[6] admittedly, holds that it is certain that the sheet was passed through the press a second time for the substitution of Y. His argument is: (*a*) Since the play was registered in 1607, its first printing was probably early in 1608; (*b*) The information on the Y title-page must refer to a performance on 1 Jan. 1608–9. But neither of these propositions is indubitably true, since (*a*) It is not impossible that for some reason there was a delay between registration and publication; and (*b*) It is not impossible that there was an earlier court-performance by the Blackfriars company, even though this has not been recorded. The Children of Paul's, for whom the play was obviously written, disappeared in the middle of 1606,[7] and the play must then have been transferred to the Children of Blackfriars, who presumably gave the

---

[4] Counting the Harvard copy, there are seven further copies with Y title-pages (six in the U.S.A. and one in Scotland): see note 15 *infra*.

[5] The copy at Eton College has a blank leaf between the title-page and A3, but this is not original, as can be seen from the chain-lines; it appears to be affixed to a stub which is the remains of the cancelled A2.

[6] W. W. Greg, *A Bibliography of the English Printed Drama to the Restoration*, vol. I, p. 395. London (Bibliographical Society) 1939. Price ("Early Editions") holds that the Y title-page was printed quite early (perhaps while sheet F was being set); that copies were never offered for sale in Elde's shop (the survival of two examples of the X title-page being an accident); and that the court performance was in 1607 or possibly 1608.

[7] E. K. Chambers, *The Elizabethan Stage* (4 vols.). II. 19–23. Oxford (Clarendon Press) 1923.

court performance referred to. Chambers[8] dates this at 1 January 1609 (which would still be 1608 by Jacobean calendar conventions), because the Blackfriars company is known to have performed at court that Christmas, whereas there is no record of their having done so the previous season. In that case, the Y title-page must have been set up during the first three months of 1609. However, it has also been argued that the court performance should be dated 1 January 1608, despite the absence of a record.[9]

In 1616, Elde printed another edition, with the following title-page:[10] A | TRICKE TO | CATCH THE | OLD ONE. | As it hath beene often in Action, | *both at Paules, the Black Fry-* | ers, and before his Maiestie. | (Rule) | By *T. Midleton*. | (Rule) | (Printer's device) | AT LONDON. | Printed by *George Eld*, for *Thomas Langley* and are | to be sold at his shop ouer against the Sarazens | Head without New-Gate. 1616. |. This looks as though it is based on the Y title-page, but adds the important information that Middleton is the author. The text that follows is a page-for-page reprint of the 1608 quarto. There is nothing in it to suggest authorial intervention: it corrects a number of mistakes in the 1608 quarto, but these are all obvious ones; and it adds many new mistakes of its own. When, therefore, I adopt readings from the 1616 edition, this is not because it has any independent authority (it hasn't), but because its emendations are ones that an editor would wish to make in any case. I have collated only one copy of the 1616 edition, that in the Victoria and Albert Museum.[11]

The authoritative text is the 1608 quarto. There is nothing in it to suggest that it was a prompt-copy or was marked for playhouse use—no instructions or advance warnings to actors or effects-men. On the contrary, there are positive signs that it was not: the minor parts are not clearly allocated or named; many exits and entrances are unmarked, and some essential stage-directions are missing; one stage-direction is "literary" rather than "theatrical"[12]; and there are small

---

[8] *Op. cit.*, III, pp. 439.

[9] G. R. Price, "The Authorship and Bibliography of *The Revenger's Tragedy*", in *The Library*, (5th series) XV (1960), p. 270 n. 2.

[10] There is an earlier state of this title, in which the commas are lacking after *Paules* and after *Fry*-ers (Greg, *op. cit.*, p. 395).

[11] The 1616 edition is probably an octavo in fours, but for convenience of reference I denote it in my textual notes by the siglum Q2. On the problems of the 1616 edition, see Price, "Early Editions", p. 225.

[12] *Trick*, IV. I. S.D.

inconsistencies in the action, which would have to be smoothed out in a production.[13] Examples of such things are pointed out in the Commentary.

The text does not show the kind of orthographical tidying-up which might be found in a scribe's fair copy; for example, there are numerous colloquial or "weak" forms, like *ath* ("on the, of the"). Many of these forms, moreover, are ones that Middleton himself used; and indeed the whole text contains large numbers of typically Middletonian spellings, such as are found in the Trinity College manuscript of *A Game at Chess*. I believe, therefore, that the 1608 quarto was set from Middleton's own autograph. Some of the evidence for this, from spellings, is given in the Appendix, p. 107.

One cannot be certain whether the printer's copy was Middleton's foul papers, or the fair copy which he had delivered to the players,[14] but the latter seems more probable, because: (*a*) Although the quarto shows some confusion between verse and prose, there is nothing in it (*e.g.* duplications, partial corrections) to suggest that it was set up from a much interlined copy; and (*b*) This play is one of several belonging to the Children of Paul's which were published in rapid succession after the company had folded up in 1606; this mass-publication suggests that the texts were disposed of by the company rather than by the individual authors.

The text of the present edition is based on the quarto of 1608, and as my copy-text I have used the British Museum copy C.34.d.42. The following silent alterations have been made: (*a*) The letter "s" has been substituted for "long s" wherever it occurs; (*b*) The complementary letters "i" and "j", "u" and "v", and "w" and "vv" have been interchanged in conformity with modern practice; (*c*) All abbreviations have been expanded; (*d*) At the end of a complete speech, where no suspension is intended, a full-point has been inserted where omitted (or where replaced by comma, semicolon, or colon); (*e*) Faulty capitalisation (at the beginning of a line of verse, or at the beginning of a proper name) has been regularised in accordance with normal Jacobean usage; (*f*) Speech-prefixes are set in caps, and are given in full and

---

[13] See, for example, the Commentary note on III. III. 33.
[14] On the existence of authorial fair copies which would be delivered to the players, but not necessarily marked for playhouse use, see Fredson Bowers, *On Editing Shakespeare and the Elizabethan Dramatists*, pp. 11ff. Philadelphia (University of Pennsylvania) 1955.

always in the same form; speech-prefixes like *1. Seru.* become FIRST SERVANT; and speech-prefixes like *1.* and *2.* (which are quite common) have been silently expanded to FIRST CREDITOR (etc.) in cases where the identity of the speaker is not in doubt; (*g*) The names of characters have been similarly normalised in stage-directions; and (*h*) Additional stage-directions, or additions to existing ones, have been provided within bent brackets.

All other departures from the copy-text are recorded in the textual notes. Where it has seemed necessary to emend punctuation, I have tried to retain the light style of punctuation characteristic of the text (and of Middleton autograph), in which the comma is the item most frequently used. I have left unchanged the Jacobean use of the question-mark both for questions and for exclamations.

The Textual Notes do not reproduce the readings of the 1616 edition or the emendations of other editors unless these have been adopted into the present text. They do however give all the substantial press-variants that I have found in the seven copies of the 1608 quarto that I have collated.[15] There are seven formes[16] which contain such press corrections: B inner, C outer, C inner, D inner, E outer, G inner, and H inner.

[15] These seven are all the copies of the 1608 quarto known to exist in England. According to Greg (*Bibliography*, p. 395) there are in addition five copies in the United States: two at the Henry E. Huntingdon Library, San Marino, California; one at the Harvard College Library, Cambridge, Mass.; one in the Carl. H. Pforzheimer Collection, New York; and one at the University of Texas, Austin, Texas. Price ("Early Editions", p. 205) lists two further copies: the Snyder-Hogan copy in the Yale University Library, and a copy in the National Library of Scotland (Bute Collection).

[16] Price ("Early Editions") reports also press-variants in B Outer, E Inner, and G Outer.

DRAMATIS PERSONAE

WITT-GOOD, *a young gentleman*

LUCRE, *his uncle*

HOORD

LAMPREY

SPICHCOCKE

SAM FREEDOME, *step-son to* LUCRE

MONYLOVE

DAMPIT, *a lawyer*

GULFE

SIR LANCELOT

ONESIPHORUS HOORD, *brother to* HOORD

KIXE

LIMBER

HOST

GEORGE, *servant to* LUCRE

ARTHUR, *servant to* HOORD

Three CREDITORS, DRAWER, BOY, VINTNER, TAYLOR, BARBER, PERFUMER, FAWLKNER, HUNTSMAN, SCRIVENER, GENTLEMEN, SERVANTS, SERJANTS

CURTIZAN

WIFE *to* LUCRE

NEECE *to* HOORD

AUDRY

LADIE FOXESTONE

⟨ACT I⟩

⟨SCENE I⟩

Enter WITT-GOOD *a Gentleman, solus.*

WITT-GOOD. ALL's gone! still thou'rt a Gentleman, that's all; but a poore one, that's nothing: What Milke brings thy Meadowes forth now? where are thy goodly Up-lands and thy Downe-lands, all sunck into that little pitte Lecherie? why should a Gallant pay but two shillings for his Ordnary that nourishes him, and twenty times two for his Brothell that consumes him? but where's Long-acre? in my Uncles conscience, which is 3. yeares voyage about; he that setts out upon his conscience, nere finds the way home againe, he is either swallowed in the quick-sands of Law-quillits, or splits upon the Piles of a Præmunire; yet these old Foxe-braind—and oxe-browde Uncles, have still defences for their Avarice, and Apologies for their practises, and will thus greete our follyes.

Hee that doth his youth expose,
To Brothell, drinke, and danger,
Let him that is his neerest Kinne,
Cheate him before a stranger.

And that's his Uncle, 'tis a principle in Usury; I dare not visit the Cittie, there I should bee too soone visited, by that horrible plague my Debts, and by that meanes I loose a Virgins love, her portion and her Vertues, well, how should a man live now, that ha's no living; hum? why are there not a million of men in the world, that onely sojourne upon their braine, and make their wittes their Mercers; and am I but one amongst that Million and cannot thrive upon't; any Trick out of the compasse of Lawe now, would come happily to me.

Enter CURTIZAN.

CURTIZAN. My love.

WITT-GOOD. My lothing; hast thou beene the secret consump-tion of my purse? and now comst to undo my last meanes, my wits? wilt leave no vertue in me and yet thou nere the better?

hence Curtizan, round webd *Tarantula*,
That dryest the Roses in the cheekes of youth.

CURTIZAN. I have beene true unto your pleasure, and all your lands thrice rackt, was never worth the Jewell which I prodigally gave you, my virginity;
Lands morgag'd may returne and more esteemde,
But honesty once pawnd, is nere redeemd.

WITT-GOOD. Forgive I do thee wrong,
To make thee sinne, and then to chide thee fort.

CURTIZAN. I know I am your loathing now, farewell.

WITT-GOOD. Stay best invention,—stay.

CURTIZAN. I that have beene the secret consumption of your purse shall I stay now to undo your last meanes, your witts? hence Curtizan away.

WITT-GOOD. I prethee, make me not mad at my owne weapon, stay, (a thing few women can do I know that, and therefore they had need weare stayes;) be not contrary, dost love me?
Fate has so cast it that all my meanes I must derive from thee.

CURTIZAN. From me! be happy then,
What lies within the power of my performance,
Shall be commanded of thee.

WITT-GOOD. Spoke like an honest drab ifaith, it may prove som-thing, what Trick is not an *Embrion* at first, until a perfect shape come over it.

CURTIZAN. Come I must helpe you, where abouts left you, Ile proceed.
Tho you beget, tis I must helpe to breed,
Speake what ist, Ide faine conceave it.

WITT-GOOD. So, so, so, thou shall presently take the name and forme upon thee of a rich country widdow foure hundred a yeare valiant, in Woods, in Bullocks, in Barnes and in Rye-stacks, weele to London, and to my covetous Uncle.

CURTIZAN. I begin to applaud thee, our States beeing both desperate, they'are soone resolute, but how for horses?

WITT-GOOD. Masse that's true, the Jest will bee of some continuance, let mee see, Horses now, a bottes on em; Stay, I have acquaintance with a madde Hoste, never yet Bawde to thee, I have rinzde the whoresons gums in Mull-sack many a time and often, put but a good Tale into his eare now, so it come off

cleanely, and there's Horse and man for us I dare warrant thee.
CURTIZAN. Arme your wittes then speedily, there shall want nothing in mee, eyther in behaviour, discourse or fashion, that shall discredit your entended purpose.
I will so art-fully disguise my wants,
And set so good a courage on my state,
That I will be beleeved.
WITT-GOOD. Why then all's furnisht; I shall goe nigh to catch that olde Foxe mine Uncle, tho hee make but some amends for my undooing, yet there's some comfort in't—hee cannot otherwise choose (tho it bee but in hope to coozen mee agen) but supply any hastie want that I bring to towne with mee, the Device well and cunningly carryed, the name of a riche Widdow, and foure hundred a yeare in good earth, will so conjure up a kinde of Usurers love in him to mee, that hee will not onely desire my presence, which at first shall scarce bee granted him, Ile keepe off a purpose, but I shall finde him so officious to deserve, so ready to supply, I know the state of an old mans affection so well, if his Nephew bee poore indeed, why hee letts God alone with him, but if hee be once rich, then heele bee the first man that helpes him.
CURTIZAN. Tis right the world, for in these dayes an olde mans love to his kindred, is like his kindnesse to his wife, 'tis alwayes done before hee comes at it.
WITT-GOOD. I owe thee for that Jest, bee gone, here's all my wealth; ⟨*Gives her his purse.*⟩ prepare thy selfe, away? Ile to mine Hoste withall possible hast, and with the best Art, and most profitable forme, powre the sweet circumstance into his eare, which shall have the gift to turne all the waxe to hunny; how now;

⟨*Enter three* GENTLEMEN.⟩

oh the right worshipful Seniors of our Country—
FIRST ⟨GENTLEMAN⟩. Whose that?
SECOND ⟨GENTLEMAN⟩. Oh the common Rioter, take no note of him.
WITT-GOOD. You will not see me now, the comfort is ere it be long you will scarce see your selves.

⟨*Exeunt* WITT-GOOD *and* CURTIZAN.⟩

First ⟨Gentleman⟩. I wonder how hee breathes, ha's consum'd all upon that Curtizan?

Second ⟨Gentleman⟩. We have heard so much.

First ⟨Gentleman⟩. You have heard all truth, his Uncle and my Brother, have beene these three yeares mortall Adversaries. Two old tough spirits, they seldome meete but fight, or quarrell when tis calmest;
I thinke their anger bee the very fire
That keepes their age alive.

Second ⟨Gentleman⟩. What was the quarrell sir?

First ⟨Gentleman⟩. Faith about a purchase, fetching over a yong heire; Maister *Hoord* my brother having wasted much time in beating the bargayne, what did me old *Lucre*, but as his conscience mov'd him, knowing the poore Gentleman, stept in betweene e'm and couzned him himselfe.

Second ⟨Gentleman⟩. And was this all sir?

First ⟨Gentleman⟩. This was e'en it sir, yet for all this I know no reason but the match might go forward betwixt his wives Sonne and my Neece, what tho there bee a dissention betweene the two olde men, I see no reason it should put a difference betweene the two yonger, tis as naturall for old folkes to fall out, as for yong to fall in? A scholler comes a wooing to my Neece, well, hee's wise, but he's poore, her Sonne comes a wooing to my Neece, well, hees a foole, but hees rich—

Second ⟨Gentleman⟩. I marry sir?

First ⟨Gentleman⟩. Pray now is not a rich foole better then a poore Philosopher.

Second ⟨Gentleman⟩. One would think so yfaith?

First ⟨Gentleman⟩. She now remaines at *London* with my brother her second Uncle, to learne fashions, practise Musicke, the voyce betweene her lips, and the violl betweene her legges, shee'le bee fitt for a consort very speedily, a thousand good pound is her portion, if she marry, weele ride up and be merry,—

Third ⟨Gentleman⟩. A match, if it be a match?

Exeunt.

⟨SCENE II⟩

Enter at one doore, Witt-good, *at the other* Host.

Witt-good. Mine Host?

HOST. Young maister *Wit-good*.
WITT-GOOD. I have beene laying all the Towne for thee.
HOST. Why what's the newes Bully-Hadland?
WITT-GOOD. What Geldings are in the house of thine owne? answer me to that first.
HOST. Why man, why?
WITT-GOOD. Marke mee what I say, Ile tell thee such a tale in thine eare, that thou shalt trust mee spite of thy teeth, furnish me with some money, wille, nille, and ride up with mee thy selfe *Contra voluntatem et professionem.*
HOST. How; let me see this trick, and Ile say thou hast more Arte then a Conjurer.
WITT-GOOD. Doost thou joy in my advancement?
HOST. Do I love Sack and Ginger?
WITT-GOOD. Comes my prosperitie desiredly to thee?
HOST. Come forfeitures to a Usurer, fees to an officer, punkes to an Hoste, and Pigs to a Parson desiredly? why then la.
WITT-GOOD. Will the report of a Widdow of foure hundred a yeare boye, make thee leape, and sing, and dance, and come to thy place agen.
HOST. Wilt thou command me now? I am thy spirit, conjure me into any shape.
WITT-GOOD. I ha brought her from her friends, turnde backe the Horses by a slight, not so much as one amongst her sixe men, goodly large Yeomanly fellowes, will shee trust with this her purpose: by this light all unmand; regardlesse of her state, neglectfull of vaine-glorious ceremonie, all for my love; oh 'tis a fine little voluble toung mine Hoste, that wins a widdow.
HOST. No 'tis a toung with a great T my boye that winnes a widdow.
WITT-GOOD. Now sir, the case stands thus, good mine Host, if thou lov'st my happinesse assist me.
HOST. Command all my beasts ith house.
WITT-GOOD. Nay thats not all neither, prethee take truce with thy joy, and listen to mee, thou know'st I have a wealthy Uncle i'th Citty, some-what the wealthier by my follyes; the report of this fortune well and cunningly carried, might be a meanes to drawe some goodnesse from the Usuring Rascall, for I have put her in hope already of some estate that I have eyther in land or

money: now if I be found true in neither, what may I expect but a suddaine breach of our love, utter dissolution of the match, and confusion of my fortunes for ever.

HOST. Wilt thou but trust the managing of thy businesse with me?

WITT-GOOD. With thee? why will I desire to thrive in my purpose, will I hugge foure hundred a yeare? I that know the misery of nothing? will that man wish a riche widdow, that has nere a hole to put his head in? with thee mine Hoste, why beleeve it, sooner with thee then with a Covy of Counsellors?

HOST. Thanke you for your good report yfaith sir, and if I stand you not insteed, why then let an Hoste come off H*ic et hæc hostis*, a deadly enemie to Dice, Drinke, and Venery; come where's this widdow?

WITT-GOOD. Hard at Parke-end.

HOST. Ile be her Serving-man for once.

WITT-GOOD. Why there wee let off together, keepe full time, my thoughts were striking then just the same number.

HOST. I knew't, shall we then see our merry dayes agen?

WITT-GOOD. ⟨*To him.*⟩ Our merry nights—⟨*Aside.*⟩ which nere shall bee more seene.

Exeunt.

⟨SCENE III⟩

Enter at severall doores, old LUCRE, *and old* HOORD, *Gentlemen* ⟨LAMPREY, SPICHCOCKE, MONYLOVE, *and* SAM FREEDOME⟩ *comming betweene them, to pacifie' em.*

LAMPREY. Nay good Maister *Lucre*, and you Maister H*oord*, anger is the winde which you're both too much troubled with-all.

HOORD. Shall my adversary thus dayly afront mee, ripping up the old wound of our malice, which three Summers could not close up, into which wound the very sight of him, drops scalding Lead insteed of Balsum.

LUCRE. Why *Hoord*, H*oord*, H*oord*, H*oord*, H*oord*; may I not passe in the state of quietnesse to mine owne house, answer mee to that, before witnesse, and why? Ile referre the cause to honest even-minded Gentlemen, or require the meere indifferences of the Lawe, to decide this matter, I got the purchase, true; was't not any mans case? yes, will a wise-man stand as a Bawd, whilst another wipes his nose of the bargaine, no, I answer no in that case.

LAMPREY. Nay sweet Maister *Lucre*.

HOORD. Was it the part of a friend: no, rather of a Jew, marke what I say, when I had beaten the bush to the last bird, or as I may terme it, the price to a pound, then like a cunning Usurer to come in the evening of the bargaine, and gleane all my hopes in a minute, to enter as it were at the back-doore of the purchase, for thou nere camst the right way by it.

LUCRE. Hast thou the conscience to tell mee so, without any impeachment to thy selfe?

HOORD. Thou that canst defeate thy owne Nephew, *Lucre*, lap his lands into bonds, and take the extremity of thy kindreds forfeitures, because hee's a rioter, a wast-thrift, a brothell-maister, and so forth—what may a Stranger expect from thee, but *Vulnera delacerata*, as the *Poet* sayes, delacerate dealing?

LUCRE. Upbraidst thou me with Nephew? is all imputation laid upon me? what acquaintance have I with his follyes, if hee riott, 'tis hee must want it, if hee surfet, 'tis hee must feele it: if he Drab it, 'tis he must lye by't, what's this to me?

HOORD. What's all to thee? nothing, nothing; such is the gulfe of thy desire, and the Wolfe of thy conscience, but be assured old Pecunious Lucre, if ever fortune so blesse me, that I may be at leisure to vexe thee, or any meanes so favour me, that I may have oportunitie to mad thee, I will pursue it with that flame of hate, that spirit of malice, unrepressed wrath, that I will blast thy comforts.

LUCRE. Ha, ha, ha!

LAMPREY. Nay maister *Hoord* you're a wise Gentleman.

HOORD. I will so crosse thee—

LUCRE. And I thee.

HOORD. So without mercy fret thee.

LUCRE. So monstrously oppose thee?

HOORD. Doost scoffe at my just anger? oh that I had as much power as usury ha's over thee?

I. III. 35. Pecunious Lucre] DILKE; pecunious lucre Q1; pecunious Lucre Q2. *From* IV. IV. 240 *it is clear that* Pecunious *is* Lucre's *christian name.*

LUCRE. Then thou wouldst have as much power as the devill ha's over thee.
HOORD. Toade!
LUCRE. Aspick.
HOORD. Serpent.
LUCRE. Viper.
SPICHCOCKE. Nay Gentlemen, then we must divide you perforce.
LAMPREY. When the fire growes too unreasonable hotte, ther's no better way then to take of the wood.

Exeunt.

Manet SAM FREEDOME *and* MONYLOVE.

SAM FREEDOME. A word good Signior.
MONYLOVE. How now, what's the newes?
SAM FREEDOME. 'Tis given mee to understand, that you are a rivall of mine in the love of Mistresse *Joyce*, maister *Hoords* Neece: say mee I, say me no.
MONYLOVE. Yes, tis so.
SAM FREEDOME. Then looke to your selfe, you cannot live long, Ime practizing every morning, a moneth hence Ile challenge you.
MONYLOVE. Give mee your hand upon't, ther's my pledge Ile meete you?

Strikes him. Exit.

SAM FREEDOME. Oh, oh—what reason had you for that sir to strike before the month, you knew I was not ready for you, and that made you so cranck, I am not such a coward to strike agen I warrant you, my eare has the lawe of her side for it burnes horribly, I will teach him to strike a naked face, the longest day of his life, slid it shall cost me some money, but Ile bring this boxe into the Chancery.

Exit.

⟨SCENE IV⟩

Enter WITT-GOOD *and the* HOST.

HOST. Feare you nothing sir, I have lodgd her in a house of credit I warrant you.
WITT-GOOD. Hast thou the writings?

68. month] Q2; mouth Q1.

HOST. Firme sir.
⟨*Enter* DAMPIT *and* GULFE.⟩
WITT-GOOD. Prethee stay, and behold two the most prodigious rascals that ever slipt into the shape of men, *Dampit* sirrah, and young *Gulfe*, his fellow Cater-piller.
HOST. *Dampit*? sure I have heard of that *Dampit*.
WITT-GOOD. Heard of him? why man he that ha's lost both his eares, may heare of him, a famous infamous Trampler of time; his owne phraze: note him well, that *Dampit* sirrah, hee in the uneven Beard, and the Serge cloake, is the most notorious, usuring, blasphemous, Atheisticall, Brothell, vomiting rascall, that wee have in these latter times now extant, whose first beginning was the stealing of a mastie Dogge from a Farmers house.
HOST. Hee lookt as if hee would obay the commandement well, when he began first with stealing.
WITT-GOOD. True, the next Towne he came at, hee set the Dogs together by'th eares.
HOST. A signe he should follow the law by my faith.
WITT-GOOD. So it followed indeed, and beeing destitute of all fortunes, stakte his Mastie against a Noble, and by great fortune his Dogge had the day, how hee made it up ten shillings I know not, but his owne boast is, that hee came to towne but with ten shillings in his purse, and now is credibly worth tenne thousand pound?
HOST. How the devill came he by it?
WITT-GOOD. How the devill came he not by it, if you put in the devill once riches come with a vengeance, has beene a Trampler of the Law sir, and the devill has a care of his footemen, the Roague has spied me now, hee nibled me finely once too a poxe search you, oh maister *Dampit*, the very Loynes of thee; crie you mercie maister *Gulfe*, you walke so lowe I promise you I sawe you not sir?
GULFE. Hee that walkes lowe walkes safe, the Poets tell us.
WITT-GOOD. ⟨*Aside.*⟩ And nyer hell by a foote and a halfe then the rest of his fellowes,
⟨*Aloud.*⟩ but my old Harry.
DAMPIT. My sweete *Theodorus*?
WITT-GOOD. Twas a merry world when thou cam'st to towne with ten shillings in thy purse.

DAMPIT. And now worth ten thousand pound my Boye, report it, H*arry Dampit*, a trampler of time, say, hee would bee up in a morning, and be here with his Serge Gowne, dasht up to the hams in a cause, have his feete stincke about *Westminster* hall and come home agen, see the Galleouns, the Galleasses, the great Armadoes of the Lawe, then there bee Hoyes and pettie vessells, Owers and Scullers of the time, there bee pick-locks of the Time too, then would I bee here, I would trample up and downe like a Mule; now to the Judges, may it please your reverend-honorable father-hoods: then to my Counsellor, may it please your worshipfull patience, then to the examiners Office, may it please your Maistershippes Gentlenesse, then to one of the Clarkes, may it please your worshipfull Lowzinesse, for I finde him scrubbing in his cod-peice, then to the hall agen, then to the Chamber agen—
WITT-GOOD. And when to the sellar agen?
DAMPIT. E'en when thou wilt agen; Tramplers of time, Motions of Fleete-streete, and Visions of Holborne, here I have fees of one, there I have fees of another, my clients come about me, the Foole-aminy and Cocks-combri of the Country, I stil trasht and trotted for other mens causes, thus was poore H*arry Dampit* made rich by others lazinesse, who, tho they would not follow their owne Suites, I made e'm follow mee with their purses.
WITT-GOOD. Did'st thou so old H*arry*?
DAMPIT. I, and I souc'st e'm with bills of Charges ifayth, twentie pound a yeare have I brought in for boate-hire, and I nere stept into boate in my life.
WITT-GOOD. Tramplers of time.
DAMPIT. I, Tramplers of time, Raskalls of time, Bulbeggars.
WITT-GOOD. Ah thou'rt a mad old H*arrie*? kinde Maister *Gulfe*, I am bould to renew my acquaintance.
GULFE. I embrace it sir.

Exeunt.

Musick

ACT II

⟨SCENE I⟩

Enter LUCRE.

LUCRE. My Adversary evermore twittes mee with my Nephew, forsooth my Nephew: why may not a vertuous uncle have a dissolute Nephewe? what tho hee bee a Brotheller, a wast-thrift, a common Surfetter, and to conclude a beggar, must sinne in him, call up shame in mee: since wee have no part in their follies, why should wee have part in their infamies? for my strickt hand toward his morgage that I denie not, I confesse I had an Uncles pennorth, let me see, halfe in halfe, true, I sawe neyther hope of his reclayming, nor comfort in his beeing, and was it not then better bestow'd upon his Uncle, then upon one of his Aunts, I neede not say bawde, for every one knowes what Aunt stands for in the last Translation—

⟨*Enter a* SERVANT.⟩

now sir.
SERVANT. Ther's a Country Serving-man sir, attends to speake with your worship.
LUCRE. Ime at best leisure now, send him in to me.

⟨*Exit* SERVANT.⟩

Enter HOST *like a Servingman.*

HOST. Blesse your venerable worship.
LUCRE. Welcome good fellow.
HOST. ⟨*Aside.*⟩ Hee calles me theefe at first sight, yet he little thinkes I am an Host?
LUCRE. What's thy busines with me?
HOST. Faith sir, I am sent from my Mistrisse to any sufficient Gentleman indeed, to aske advise upon a doubtfull point, 'tis indifferent sir, to whome I come, for I know none, nor did my Mistres direct mee to any perticuler man, for shee's as meere a stranger here as my selfe, onely I found your worship within, and tis a thing I ever lov'd sir to be dispacht as soone as I can.

Lucre. ⟨*Aside.*⟩ A good blunt honesty, I like him wel,
⟨*Aloud.*⟩ what is thy Mistres?

Host. Fayth a Cuntry Gentlewoman and a widdow sir, yesterday was the first flight of us, but now shee entends to stay till a little Tearme businesse be ended.

Lucre. Her name I prethee?

Host. It runnes there in the writings sir, among her Lands, widdow Medler?

Lucre. Medler? masse have I neere heard of that widdow?

Host. Yes, I warrant you, have you sir, not the rich widdowe in *Staffordsheere?*

Lucre. Cuds me, there tis indeede, thou hast put me into memorie, there's a widdow indeed, ah that I were a batchiler agen.

Host. No doubt your worship might do much then, but she's fayrely promist to a bachiler already.

Lucre. Ah what is he I prethee?

Host. A Country Gentleman too, one whome your worship knowes not Ime sure: has spent some fewe follies in his youth, but marriage by my fayth begins to call him home, my Mistris loves him sir, and love covers faults you know, one maister *Wit-good* if ever you have heard of the Gentleman.

Lucre. Ha? *Wit-good* sayst thou?

Host. Thats his name indeede sir; my Mistris is like to bring him to a goodly seate yonder, foure hundred a yeare by my faith.

Lucre. But I pray take me with you.

Host. I sir?

Lucre. What Countryman might this yong *Wit-good* be?

Host. A *Lestershire* gentleman sir.

Lucre. ⟨*Aside.*⟩ My Nephew, by th masse my Nephew, Ile fetch out more of this yfaith, a simple Country fellow, Ile workte out of him, ⟨*Aloud.*⟩ and is that Gentleman sayst thou presently to marrie her?

Host. Fayth he brought her up to towne sir, has the best card in all the bunch fort, her heart: and I know my Mistris will bee married, ere she goe downe, nay Ile sweare that, for she's none of those widdowes that will goe downe first, and bee married after, she hates that I can tell you sir.

Lucre. By my faith sir, shee is like to have a proper Gentleman and a comelie, Ile give her that gift?

HOST. Why do's your worship know him sir?
LUCRE. I know him! dos not all the world knowe him, can a man of such exquisite qualities be hid under a bushell?
HOST. Then, your worshippe may save mee a labour, for I had charge given me to enquire after him.
LUCRE. Enquire of him? if I might counsell thee, thou shouldst nere trouble thy selfe furder, enquire of him of no more but of mee, Ile fit thee? I grant he has beene youthfull, but is he not now reclaimde; marke you that sir, has not your Mistris thinke you beene wanton in her youth? if men bee wagges, are there not women wagtayles?
HOST. No doubt sir.
LUCRE. Do's not he returne wisest, that comes home whipt with his owne follies.
HOST. Why very true sir.
LUCRE. The worst report you can heare of him I can tell you is that hee has beene a kinde Gentleman, a liberall and a worthie, who but lustie W*it-good*, thrice Noble W*it-good*.
HOST. Since your worshippe has so much knowledge in him, can you resolve me Sir what his living might bee, my duty bindes me sir to have a care of my mistris estate, she has beene ever a good mistris to me though I say it, many welthy Suiters has shee Nonsuted for his sake, yet tho her Love bee so fixt, a man cannot tell whether his Non-performance may helpe to remove it sir; hee makes us beleeve hee has lands and living.
LUCRE. Who young maister *Wit-good*! why beleeve it he has as goodly a fine living out yonder, what do you call the place?
HOST. Nay I know not ifaith.
LUCRE. Hum, see like a Beast if I have not forgot the name, puh, and out yonder agen, goodly growen woods and faire meadowes, pax ont, I can nere hit of that place neither, hee; why hes W*it-good* of W*it-good-Hall*, hee, an unknowe thing.
HOST. Is he so sir, to see how rumor will alter, trust me sir we heard once he had no lands, but all lay morgagde to an Uncle he has in towne here.
LUCRE. Push, tis a tale, tis a tale.
HOST. I can assure you sir twas credibly reported to my Mistris.
LUCRE. Why doe you thinke ifaith hee was ever so simple to morgage his lands to his Uncle? or his uncle so unnaturall to take

the extremity of such a morgage.

Host. That was my saying still sir.

Lucre. Puh, nere thinke it.

Host. Yet that report goes currant.

Lucre. Nay then you urge me,
Cannot I tell that best that am his Uncle.

Host. How sir! what have I donne.

Lucre. Why how now in a Sowne, man.

Host. Is your worship his Uncle sir.

Lucre. Can that be any harme to you sir.

Host. I do beseech you sir do me the favour to conceale it, what a Beast was I to utter so much: pray sir doe mee the kindnesse to keepe it in, I shall have my coate pull'd ore my eares, ant should bee knowne, for the truth is an't please your worshippe, to prevent much rumour and many suiters, they entend to bee married verie suddenly and privately.

Lucre. And do'st thou thinke it stands with my Judgement to doe them injury, must I needes say the knowledge of this marriage comes from thee? am I a foole at fifty foure? doe I lacke subteltie now that have got all my wealth by it? there's a leash of Angells for thee, come let mee wo thee, speake where lie they?

Host. So I might have no anger sir—

Lucre. Passion of me not a jot, prethe come.

Host. I would not have it knowne it came by my meanes,—

Lucre. Why am I a man of wisdome?

Host. I dare trust your worship sir, but I'me a stranger to your house, and to avoyde al Intelligencers I desire your worshippes eare.

Lucre. ⟨*Aside.*⟩ This fellowe's worth a matter of trust—
⟨*Aloud.*⟩ come sir, why now thou'rt an honest lad:

⟨Host *whispers to him.*⟩

ah sirrah Nephew?

Host. Please you sir now I have begunne with your worship when shall I attend, for your advice upon that doubtfull poynt, I must come warily now.

Lucre. Tut, feare thou nothing, to morrowes evening shall resolve the doubt.

Host. The time shall cause my attendance. *Exit.*

LUCRE. Fare thee well: there's more true honesty in such a Cuntrie Servingman, then in a hundred of our cloake companions, I may well call e'm companions, for since blew coates have beene turn'd into cloakes, wee can scarce knowe the man from the Maister—*George*—

⟨*Enter* GEORGE.⟩

GEORGE. Anon sir?
LUCRE. List hether,—

⟨*Whispers to him.*⟩

keepe the place secret, commend mee to my Nephewe, I knowe no cause tell him but hee might see his Uncle?
GEORGE. I will sir.
LUCRE. And doe you heare sir, take heede you use him with respect and duty.
GEORGE. ⟨*Aside.*⟩ Here's a strange alteration, one day he must be turnd out like a Beggar, and now he must be cald in like a Knight! *Exit.*
LUCRE. Ah Sirrah, that rich widdow, 400. a yeare, beside I here she layes Clayme to a title of a hundred more, this falls unhappily that he should beare a Grudge to me now being likely to prove so rich, what ist tro that hee makes me a Stranger for? hum, I hope he has not so much wit to apprehend that I cozned him, he deceaves me then? good heaven, who would have thought, it would ever have come to this passe,—yet hee's a proper Gentleman ifaith, give him his due—marry thats his Morgage, but that I nere meane to give him, ile make him rich inough in words if that be good, and if it come to a peece of mony I will not greatly sticke fort, there may be hope some of the widdowes lands too, may one day fall upon me if things be carried wisely:

⟨*Enter* GEORGE.⟩

now sir, where is he?
GEORGE. He desires your worship to hold him excusde, he has such weighty Busines it commands him wholy from all men.
LUCRE. Were those my Nephewes words?
GEORGE. Yes indeed sir.

LUCRE. When men grow rich they grow proud too, I perceive that, he would not have sent me such an answere once within this twelvemonth, see what tis when a mans come to his lands, returne to him agen sir, tell him his Uncle desires his company for an hower, Ile trouble him but an hower say, tis for his owne good tell him, and do you heare sir, put worship upon him, go too, doe as I bid you, he's like to be a Gentleman of worship very shortly.

GEORGE. ⟨*Aside.*⟩ This is good sport ifaith. *Exit.*

LUCRE. Troth he uses his Uncle, discourteously now, can he tell what I may do for him, Goodnes may come from me in a minute that comes not in Seaven yeare agen, hee knowes my humour, I am not so usually good, tis no small thing that drawes kindnes from me, he may know that, and he will; the cheife cause that invites me to do him most good, is the suddaine astonishing of ould Hoord my Adversary, how pale his malice will looke at my Nephewes Advancement, with what a dejected Spirit hee will behold his Fortunes, whome but last day, hee proclaymde Riotter, Penurious Make-shift, dispised Brothell Maister; ha, ha, twill doe me more secret Joy then my last purchasse, more pretious comfort then all these widdowes Revennewes,—

Enter ⟨GEORGE *and*⟩ WITT-GOOD.

Now Sir.—

GEORGE. With much entrety he's at length come sir.

LUCRE. Oh Nephew, let me salute you sir, your welcome Nephew.

WITT-GOOD. Uncle I thanke you.

LUCRE. Yave a fault Nephew, your a Stranger here, well Heaven give you joy.

WITT-GOOD. Of what Sir?

LUCRE. Hah, we can heare.
  You might have knowne your Uncles house ifaith,
  You and your widdow, go too, you were too blame;
  If I may tell you so without offence.

WITT-GOOD. How could you heare of that sir?

LUCRE. Oh pardon me,
  It was your will to have it kept from me I perceive now.

WITT-GOOD. Not for any defect of Love I protest Uncle.

LUCRE. Oh twas Unkindnes Nephew, fie, fie, fie.

Witt-good. I am sory you take it in that sence sir.
Lucre. Puh, you cannot coulour it ifaith Nephew.
Witt-good. Will you but heare what I can say in my just excuse sir.
Lucre. Yes faith will I, and welcome.
Witt-good. You that know my danger ith Citty sir so well, how great my debts are, and how extreame my Creditors could not out of your pure judgment sir, have wisht us hether.
Lucre. Masse a firme reason indeed.
Witt-good. Else my Uncles house, why tad beene the onely make-Match.—
Lucre. Nay and thy credit.
Witt-good. My credit? nay my countenance, push, nay I know uncle you would have wrought it so by your wit you would have made her beleeve in time the whole house had beene mine—
Lucre. I and most of the goods too—
Witt-good. La you there; wel, let e'm al prate what they will ther's nothing like the bringing of a widdow to ones Uncles house.
Lucre. Nay let Nephewes be rulde as they list, they shall finde their Uncles house, the most naturall place when all's done.
Witt-good. There they may be bold.
Lucre. Life, they may do any thing there man, and feare neither Beadle nor Somner, an Uncles house! a very coale-harbour? Sirra, Ile touch thee neere now, hast thou so much interest in thy widdow, that by a token thou couldst presently send for her?
Witt-good. Troth I thinke I can uncle.
Lucre. Go too, let me see that?
Witt-good. Pray command one of your men hether Uncle.
Lucre. George?
George. Here sir.
Lucre. Attend my Nephew?

⟨Witt-good *speaks aside to* George.⟩

I love a life to prattle with a rich widdow, tis pretty me thinkes when our tongues goe togither, and then to promise much and performe little; I love that sport a life yfaith, yet I am in the moode now to do my Nephew some good, if he take me handsomely:

⟨*Exit* GEORGE.⟩

what have you dispacht?
WITT-GOOD. I ha sent sir?
LUCRE. Yet I must condemne you of unkindnesse Nephew.
WITT-GOOD. Heaven forbid Uncle?
LUCRE. Yes fayth must I; say your debts bee many, your creditors importunate, yet the kindnesse of a thing is all Nephew, you might have sent me close word on't, without the least danger, or præjudice to your fortunes.
WITT-GOOD. Troth I confesse it Uncle, I was too blame there, but indeed my intent was to have clapt it up suddainely, and so have broke forth like a joye to my friends, and a wonder to the world, beside there's a trifle of a forty pound matter towarde the setting of mee forth, my friends should nere have knowne on't, I meant to make shift for that my selfe.
LUCRE. How Nephew? let me not heare such a word agen, I beseech you,—shall I be beholding to you?
WITT-GOOD. To me alasse, what do you meane Uncle?
LUCRE. I charge you upon my love: you trouble no body but my selfe.
WITT-GOOD. Y'ave no reason for that Uncle.
LUCRE. Troth Ile nere bee friends with you while you live and you doe.
WITT-GOOD. Nay and you say so Uncle, here's my hand, I will not doote—
LUCRE. Why well sayde, there's some hope in thee when thou wilt bee rulde, ile make it up fifty fayth, because I see thee so reclaimde;

⟨*Enter Lucre's* WIFE *and* SAM FREEDOME.⟩

peace, here comes my wife with *Sam* her tother husbands Sonne.
WITT-GOOD. Good Aunt—
SAM FREEDOME. Couzen *Wit-good*? I rejoyce in my salute, your most welcome to this Noble Citty govern'd with the sword in the Scabbard.
WITT-GOOD. ⟨*Aside.*⟩ And the wit in the pommell,
⟨*Aloud.*⟩ good Maister *Sam Fredome* I returne the salute.

LUCRE. By the masse she's comming wife, let mee see now how thou wilt entertaine her. 285
WIFE. I hope I am not to learne sir, to entertaine a widdowe, tis not so long ago since I was one my selfe?

⟨*Enter* CURTIZAN.⟩

WITT-GOOD. Uncle?
LUCRE. Shee's come indeed?
WITT-GOOD. My Uncle was desirous to see you widdow, and I præsum'd to envite you. 290
CURTIZAN. The præsumption was nothing Maister W*it-good*, is this your Uncle sir?
LUCRE. Marry am I sweete widdow, and his good Uncle he shal finde me, I by this smack that I give thee, thou'rt welcome, 295

⟨*Kisses her.*⟩

wife, bid the widdow welcome the same way agen.
SAM FREEDOME. ⟨*Aside.*⟩ I am a Gentleman now too, by my fathers occupation, and I see no reason but I may kisse a widdowe by my Fathers Coppy, truely I thinke the Charter is not against it, surely these are the wordes, the Sonne once a Gentleman, 300 may revell it, tho his father were a dauber, tis about the 15 page,—ile to her—

⟨*Attempts to kiss* CURTIZAN, *but is rebuffed.*⟩

LUCRE. Y'are not very busie now, a worde with thee sweete widdow—

⟨*Talks with her aside.*⟩

SAM FREEDOME. Coades-Nigs, I was never so disgrac'st, since 305 the houre my mother whipt me.
LUCRE. Beside, I have no childe of mine owne to care for, shee's my second wife, old, past bearing, clap sure to him widdow, he's like to be my heire I can tell you?
CURTIZAN. Is he so sir? 310
LUCRE. Hee knowes it already and the knaves proud on't, jolly rich widdowes have beene offerd him here ith Citty, great marchants wives, and do you thinke he would once looke upon e'm? forsooth heele none, you are beholding to him ith Country

then, ere we could be, nay, ile hold a wager widdow if hee were
once knowne to bee in towne, hee would bee presently sought
after, nay and happie were they, that could catch him first.

CURTIZAN. I thinke so?

LUCRE. Oh, there would be such running to and fro widdow,
hee should not passe the streetes for e'm: he'ed bee tooke up in
one great house or other presently, fah, they know he has it and
must have it; you see this house here widdowe, this house and all
comes to him, goodly Roomes ready furnisht, seeld with plaster
of paris, and all hung about with cloth of arras. Nephew!

WITT-GOOD. Sir—

LUCRE. Shew the widdowe your house, carry her into all the
Roomes, and bid her welcome,—you shall see widdow—

⟨*Takes* WITT-GOOD *aside.*⟩

Nephew?—strike all sure above and thou bee'st a good boye—
ah—

WITT-GOOD. Alasse sir, I know not how shee would take it.

LUCRE. The right way I warrant tee, a poxe, art an asse, would I
were in thy stead, get you up, I am a shamde of you,

⟨*Exeunt* WITT-GOOD *and* CURTIZAN.⟩

⟨*Aside.*⟩ so: let e'm agree as they wil now? many a match has
beene struck up in my house a this fashion, let e'm try all
manner of waies still there's nothing like an Uncles house to
strike the stroake in,—Ile hold my wife in talke a little,

⟨*Aloud.*⟩ now *Ginnee*; your sonne there goes a wooing to a poore
Gentlewoman but of a 1000. portion, see my Nephew, a lad of
lesse hope, strikes at foure hundred a yeare in good Rubbish.

WIFE. Well we must do as we may sir.

LUCRE. ⟨*Aside.*⟩ Ile have his money ready told for him, againe
hee come downe, let mee see too, by'th masse I must present
the widdowe with some Jewell, a good peece a plate or such a
device, twill harten her on wel, I have a very faire standing cup,

---

II. I. 324. about] Q2; aboue Q1. *Misreading of* t *as* e *by* Q1 *compositor. An arras was hung round the walls, not "above"; it is hardly likely that* Q1 *aboue could mean "upstairs".*

and a good hie standing cup will please a widow above al other peices.

Exit.

WIFE. Do you mock us with your Nephew, I have a plot in my head sonne, ifaith husband to crosse you.

SAM FREEDOME. Is it a tragedy plot, or a comedy plot, good mother.

WIFE. Tis a plot shall vexe him, I charge you of my blessing Sonne *Sam*, that you presently withdrawe the Action of your love from Maister H*oords* Neece.

SAM FREEDOME. How mother.

WIFE. Nay I have a plot in my head ifaith, here take this chain of gold and this faire diamond, dogge me the widdow home to her lodging, and at thy best opportunity fasten e'm both upon her—nay I have a Reach, I can tell you thou art knowne what thou art sonne among the right worshipfull; all the twelve companyes.

SAM FREEDOME. Truely I thanke 'em for it.

WIFE. He, he's a scab to thee, and so certifie her, thou hast two hundred a yeare of thy selfe, beside thy good parts—a proper person and a lovely, if I were a widdow I could find in my heart to have thee my selfe, sonne, I, from em all.

SAM FREEDOME. Thanke you for your good will mother, but in deed I had rather have a Stranger: and if I wo her not in that Violent fashion, that I will make her bee glad to take these gifts ere I leave her, let me never be called the heire of your body.

WIFE. Nay I know theres inough in you sonne if you once come to put it forth.

SAM FREEDOME. Ile quickly make a Bolt, or a shaft ont.

Exeunt.

⟨SCENE II⟩

Enter HOORD *and* MONYLOVE.

MONYLOVE. Faith Maister *Hoord*, I have bestowde many months in the Suite of your Neece, such was the deere love I ever bore to her vertues, but since she hath so extreamely denied me, I am to lay out for my fortunes else where.

HOORD. Heaven forbid but you should sir, I ever told you my
Neece, stood otherwise affected.

MONYLOVE. I must confesse you did sir, yet in regard of my great
losse of time, and the zeale with which I sought your Neece,
shall I desire one favour of your worship.

HOORD. In regard of those two tis hard but you shall sir.

MONYLOVE. I shall rest gratefull, tis not full 3. houres sir, since
the happy rumour of a rich Country widdow came to my
hearing.

HOORD. How a rich Country widdow?

MONYLOVE. Foure hundred a yeare landed.

HOORD. Yea?

MONYLOVE. Most firme sir, and I have learnt her lodging, here
my suite begins sir, if I might but entreate your worship to bee a
countenance for mee, and speake a good word: for your words
will passe, I nothing doubt, but I might set faire for the widdowe,
nor shall your labour sir end altogither in thankes, two hundred
Angells—

HOORD. So, so, what suiters has shee?

MONYLOVE. There lies the comfort sir, the report of her is yet
but a whisper, and onely sollicited by young Riotous *Wit-good*,
Nephew to your mortall adversary.

HOORD. Ha? art certaine he's her suiter?

MONYLOVE. Most certaine sir, and his Uncle very industrious to
beguile the widdow, and make up the match!

HOORD. So? very good?

MONYLOVE. Now sir you know this yong *Wit-good* is a spend-
thrift—dissolute fellow.

HOORD. A very Raskall.

MONYLOVE. A mid-night surfetter.

HOORD. The spume of a Brothel-house.

MONYLOVE. True sir? which beeing well told in your worshippes
phraze, may both heave him out of her minde, and drive a faire
way for me to the widdowes affections.

HOORD. Attend me about 5.

MONYLOVE. With my best care sir. *Exit.*

HOORD. Foole thou hast left thy treasure with a theefe, to trust
a widdower with a suite in love, happy revenge I hug thee, I have
not onely the meanes layde before me, extreamely to crosse my

adversary, and confound the last hopes of his Nephew, but ther-by to enrich my state; augment my revennewes, and build mine owne fortunes greater, ha, ha.
Ile marre your phraze, ore-turne your flatteries,
Undo your windings, policies, and plots,
Fall like a secret and dispatchfull plauge on your secured comforts,
why I am able to buy 3. of *Lucre*, thrice out-bid him, let my out-monies be reckond and all.

Enter three CREDITORS.

FIRST CREDITOR. I am glad of this newes.
SECOND CREDITOR. So are we by my faith.
THIRD CREDITOR. Yong *Wit-good* will be a gallant agen now.
HOORD. Peace?
FIRST CREDITOR. I promise you Maister Cock-pit she's a mighty rich widdow.
SECOND CREDITOR. Why have you ever heard of her?
FIRST CREDITOR. Who widdow Medler, shee lies open to much rumour.
THIRD CREDITOR. Foure hundred a yeare they say in very good land.
FIRST CREDITOR. Nay tak't of my word if you beleeve that, you beleeve the least.
SECOND CREDITOR. And to see how closse hee keepes it.
FIRST CREDITOR. Oh sir there's policy in that to prevent better suiters.
THIRD CREDITOR. Hee owes me a hundred pound, and I protest I neere lookte for a pennie.
FIRST CREDITOR. He little dreames of our comming, heele wonder to see his creditors upon him.

Exeunt ⟨CREDITORS⟩.

HOORD. Good, his creditors, ile follow, this makes for mee, all know the widdowes wealth and tis well knowne, I can estate her fairely, I and will.
In this one chance shines a twice happy Fate,
I both deject my foe, and raise my state.

Exit.

Musick

ACT III

⟨SCENE I⟩

⟨*Enter*⟩ WITT-GOOD *with his* CREDITORS.

WITT-GOOD. Why alasse, my Creditors? could you finde no other time to undo mee but now, rather your malice appeares in this then the justnesse of the debt.

FIRST CREDITOR. Maister W*it-good* I have forborne my money long.

WITT-GOOD. I pray speake lowe sir, what do you meane?

SECOND CREDITOR. We heare you are to be married suddainely to a rich Country widdow?

WITT-GOOD. What can bee kept so closse but you creditors here on't, wel, tis a lamentable state, that our cheifest afflicters should first heare of our fortunes, why this is no good course yfaith sirs, if ever you have hope'to bee satisfied, why doe you seeke to confound the meanes that should worke it, there's neither piety, no nor policy in that, shine favorably now, why I may rize and spred agen, to your great comforts.

FIRST CREDITOR. He saies true yfaith.

WITT-GOOD. Remove me now, and I consume for ever.

SECOND CREDITOR. Sweete Gentleman?

WITT-GOOD. How can it thrive which from the Sun you sever.

THIRD CREDITOR. It cannot indeed?

WITT-GOOD. Oh then show patience, I shall have ynough to satisfie you all.

FIRST CREDITOR. I, if we could be content a shame take us.

WITT-GOOD. For looke you, I am but newly sure yet to the widdow, and what a Rend might this discredit make: within these 3. daies will I binde you lands for your securities.

FIRST CREDITOR. No, good Maister *Wit-good*,
Would twere as much as we dare trust you with?

WITT-GOOD. I know you have beene kinde, how ever now either by wrong report, or false incitement your gentlenesse is injurde, in such a state as this a man cannot want foes.
If on the suddaine he begin to rize,

No man that lives can count his enimyes.
You had some intelligence I warrant yee, from an ill-willer.
SECOND CREDITOR. Faith wee heard you brought up a rich widdow sir, and were suddainely to marry her.
WITT-GOOD. I, why there it was, I knew twas so, but since you are so wel resolvde of my faith toward you, let me be so much favor'd of you, I beseech you all—
ALL. Oh, it shall not need ifaith sir,—
WITT-GOOD. As to lie still a while, and bury my debts in silence, till I be fully possest of the widdow, for the truth is, I may tell you as my friends—
ALL. Oh—o—o—
WITT-GOOD. I am to raise a little money in the Citty, toward the setting forth of my selfe, for mine owne credit, and your comfort, now if my former debts should be divulg'd, all hope of my proceedings were quite extinguisht!

⟨FIRST CREDITOR *takes* WITT-GOOD *aside*.⟩

FIRST CREDITOR. Do you heare sir, I may deserve your custome heereafter, pray let my money be accepted before a strangers, here's fortie pound I receiv'd as I came to you, if that may stand you in any stead make use on't, nay pray sir, tis at your service—
WITT-GOOD. You doe so ravish mee with kindnesse, that I'me constrainde, to play the maide and take it?
FIRST CREDITOR. Let none of them see it I beseech you.
WITT-GOOD. Fah—
FIRST CREDITOR. I hope I shall be first in your remembrance after the marriage rites.
WITT-GOOD. Beleeve it firmely.
FIRST CREDITOR. So,
  ⟨*Aloud.*⟩ what do you walke sirs?
SECOND CREDITOR. I goe—

⟨*Takes* WITT-GOOD *aside.*⟩

take no care sir for money to furnish you, within this houre ile send you sufficient:
  ⟨*Aloud.*⟩ come Maister Cock-pit wee both stay for you.

THIRD CREDITOR. I ha lost a ring ifaith, ile followe you presently—

⟨*Exeunt* FIRST *and* SECOND CREDITORS.⟩

but you shall finde it sir, I know your youth and expences have disfurnisht you of all Jewells, ther's a Ruby of twenty pound price sir, bestowe it upon your widdow,—what man, twill call up her bloud to you, beside if I might so much worke with you, I would not have you beholding to those bloud-suckers for any money.

WITT-GOOD. Not I beleeve it.

THIRD CREDITOR. The'ar a brace of cut-throates?

WITT-GOOD. I know e'm.

THIRD CREDITOR. Send a note of all your wants to my shoppe and ile supply you instantly.

WITT-GOOD. Say you so, why here's my hand then, no man living shal do't but thy selfe.

THIRD CREDITOR. Shall I carry it away from e'm both then?

WITT-GOOD. Ifaith shalt thou?

THIRD CREDITOR. Troth then I thanke you sir.

WITT-GOOD. Welcome good maister Cock-pit!

Exit ⟨THIRD CREDITOR⟩.

ha, ha, ha? why is not this better now, then lying a bed, I perceive there's nothing conjures up wit sooner then poverty, and nothing laies it downe sooner then wealth and lecherie? this has some savour yet, oh that I had the morgage from mine Uncle as sure in possession as these trifles, I would forsweare Brothel at noone day, and Muscadine and eggs at midnight.

Enter CURTIZAN.

CURTIZAN. Maister W*it-good*? where are you?
WITT-GOOD. Holla.
CURTIZAN. Rich Newes!
WITT-GOOD. Would twere all in Plate.
CURTIZAN. There's some in chaines and Jewells, I am so haunted with shuters Maister W*it-good*, I know not which to dispatch first.
WITT-GOOD. You have the better tearme by my faith.

Curtizan. Among the number, one Maister H*oord* an Antient Gentleman.
Witt-good. Upon my life my Uncles adversary.
Curtizan. It may well hold so, for he rayles on you, Speakes shamefully of him.
Witt-good. As I could wish it.
Curtizan. I first denyed him, but so cunningly, It rather promisde him assured hopes, Then any losse of labour.
Witt-good. Excellent.
Curtizan. I expect him every hower, with Gentlemen, With whome he labours to make good his words, To approve you Riotous, your state consumde, your Uncle,—
Witt-good. Wench, make up thy owne fortunes now, do thy selfe a good turne once in thy Dayes, hees rich in money, moveables, and lands,—marry him, he's an old doting foole, and thats worth all, marry him, twould bee a great comfort to me to see thee do well ifaith,—marry him, twould ease my conscience well to see thee well bestowd, I have a care of thee ifaith.
Curtizan. Thankes sweete maister W*it-good.*
Witt-good. I reach at farder happines; first I am sure it can be no harme to thee, and there may happen goodnes to me by it, prosecute it well, lets send up for our witts, now we require their best and most pregnant Assistance!
Curtizan. Step in, I thinke I heare e'm. *Exeunt.*

Enter Hoord *and* Gentlemen *with the* Host ⟨*as*⟩ *servingman.*

Hoord. Art thou the widdowes man, by my faith sh'as a company of proper men then.
Host. I am the worst of sixe sir, good inough for blew-coates.
Hoord. Harke hether, I heare say thou art in most credit with her.
Host. Not so sir.
Hoord. Come, come, thou'rt modest, theres a Brace of royalls, prethee helpe me to'th speech of her.
Host. Ile do what I may sir alwayes saving my selfe harmelesse.
Hoord. Go too do't I say, thou shalt heare better from me.

HOST. ⟨*Aside.*⟩ Is not this a better place then 5. Marke a yeare standing wages; say a man had but 3. such clients in a day, me thinkes he might make a poore living ont, beside I was never brought up with so little honesty, to refuse any mans mony never; what gulles there are a this side the world, now knowe I the widdowes minde, none but my yong master comes in her clutches, ha, ha, ha. *Exit.*

HOORD. Now my deere Gentlemen stand firmely to me, you know his follyes, and my worth.

FIRST GENTLEMAN. Wee doo sir.

SECOND GENTLEMAN. But Maister Hoord, are you sure he is not ith house now?

HOORD. Upon my honesty I chose this time,
A purpose, fit, the spend-thrift is abroad,
Assist me: here she comes:

⟨*Enter* CURTIZAN. WITT-GOOD *watches from concealment.*⟩

now my sweete widdow—

CURTIZAN. Yare wellcome Maister Hoord.

HOORD. Dispatch, sweet Gentlemen, dispatch,
I am come widdow, to prove those my words,
Neither of envy Sprung nor of false tongs,
But such as their desarts and Actions,
Doe merit and bring forth, all which these Gentlemen
well knowne and better reputted will confesse.

CURTIZAN. I cannot tell,
How my affections may dispose of me,
But surely if they find him so desartlesse,
Theyle have that reason to with-draw them-selves.
And therefore Gentlemen I doe entreat you,
As you are faire in Reputation,
And in appearing forme so shine in truth;
I am a widdow and alasse you knowe,
Soone overthrowen, tis a very small thing,
That we with-stand, our weakenes is so great,
Be partiall unto neither, but deliver,
Without affection your opinion.

HOORD. And that will drive it home.

CURTIZAN. Nay I beseech your silence Maister Hoord,
   You are a party.
HOORD. Widdow? not a word!
FIRST GENTLEMAN. The better first to worke you to beleife,
   Know neither of us owe him flattery,
   Nor tother malice, but unbribed censure,
   So helpe us our best fortunes.
CURTIZAN. It suffizes?
FIRST GENTLEMAN. That W*it-good* is a riotous undon man,
   Imperfect both in fame and in estate:
   His debts welthier then he, and executions
   In waite for his due body, we'ele maintayne
   With our best credit, and our deerest bloud.
CURTIZAN. Nor land, nor living say you, pray take heede you do
   not wrong the Gentleman?
FIRST GENTLEMAN. What we speake,
   Our lives and meanes are ready to make good.
CURTIZAN. Alasse, how soone are wee poore soules beguild!
SECOND GENTLEMAN. And for his Uncle.—
HOORD. Let that come to me,
   His Uncle a severe extortioner,
   A Tyrant at a forfeiture, greedy of others miseries,
   One that would undo his brother; nay swallowe
   Up his father, if he can
   Within the fadomes of his conscience.
FIRST GENTLEMAN. Nay beleeve it widdow,
   You had not onely matcht your selfe to wants,
   But in an evill and unnaturall stocke.
HOORD. Follow hard, Gentlemen, follow hard?
CURTIZAN. Is my love so deceav'd, before you all
   I do renounce him, on my knees I vow
   He nere shall marry mee,—
WITT-GOOD. ⟨*Aside.*⟩ Heaven knowes hee never meant it?
HOORD. There, take her at the bound,—
FIRST GENTLEMAN. Then with a new and pure affection,
   Behold yon Gentleman, grave, kinde and rich:
   A match worthy your selfe, esteeming him,
   You do regard your state.
HOORD. Ile make her a joynture say.

First Gentleman. Hee can joyne land to land, and will possesse you of what you can desire.
Second Gentleman. Come widdow come.
Curtizan. The world is so deceitfull?
First Gentleman. There tis deceitfull,
Where flattery, want, and imperfection lies:
But none of these in him? push—
Curtizan. Pray sir—
First Gentleman. Come you widdowes are ever most backward, when you should doe your selves most good, but were it to marry a chin not worth a haire now, then you would bee forward ynough? come, clap hands, a match.
Hoord. Withall my heart widdow, thankes Gentlemen,
I will deserve your labour, and thy love.
Curtizan. Alasse, you love not widdowes but for wealth,
I promise you I ha nothing sir.
Hoord. Well said, widdowe, well said, thy Love is all I seeke, before these Gentlemen.
Curtizan. Now I must hope the best.
Hoord. My joyes are such they want to be exprest.
Curtizan. But Maister H*oord*, one thing I must remember you of before these gentlemen your friends, how shall I suddainly avoyde the loathed Solleciting of that perjurd W*it-good*, and his Tedious-dissembling Uncle, who this very day hath appointed a meeting for the same purpose too, where had not truth come forth I had beene undon, utterly undon.
Hoord. What thinke you of that Gentlemen.
First Gentleman. Twas well devized.
Hoord. Harke thee widdow, trayne out yong W*it-good* single, hasten him thether with thee, somewhat before the hower where at the place appointed these Gentlemen and my selfe wil waite the opportunty, when by some slieght removing him from thee we'le suddenly enter and surprise thee, carry thee away by boate to Coale-harbour, have a Priest ready and there Clap it up instantly, how lik'st it widdow?
Curtizan. In that it pleaseth you, it likes me well.
Hoord. Ile kisse thee for those words, come Gentlemen,
Still must I live a Suiter to your favours,
Still to your aide beholding.

FIRST GENTLEMAN. We're engagde sir.
  Tis for our credits now to see't well ended. 250
HOORD. Tis for your honors Gentlemen; nay looke toote,
  Not onely in joy, but I in wealth excell,
  No more sweet widdow, but sweete wife, farwell.
CURTIZAN. Farwell sir.—

Exeunt ⟨HOORD *and* GENTLEMEN⟩.

Enter WITT-GOOD.

WITT-GOOD. Oh for more scope, I could laugh eternally, 255
  Give you joye Mistres *Hoord*, I promise your fortune was good
  forsooth, y'ave fell upon wealth ynough, and there's young
  Gentlemen enow can helpe you to the rest; now it requires our
  wits: carry thy selfe but heedfully now, and wee are both—

⟨*Enter* HOST.⟩

HOST. Maister W*it-good* your Uncle— 260

Enter LUCRE.

WITT-GOOD. Cuds me, remove thy selfe a while, ile serve for
  him?

⟨*Exeunt* CURTIZAN *and* HOST.⟩

LUCRE. Nephew, good morrow, Nephew?
WITT-GOOD. The same to you kinde Uncle.
LUCRE. How fares the widdow, do's the meeting hold? 265
WITT-GOOD. Oh no question of that sir?
LUCRE. Ile strike the stroake then for thee, no more daies.
WITT-GOOD. The sooner the better Uncle, oh shee's mightily
  followed,—
LUCRE. And yet so little rumourd. 270
WITT-GOOD. Mightily? here comes one old Gentleman, and
  heele make her a joynture of three hundred a yeare forsooth,
  another welthy suiter wil estate his sonne in his life time, and make
  him weigh downe the widdow, here a Merchants sonne will
  possesse her with no lesse then three goodly Lordships at once, 275
  which were all pawnes to his Father.
LUCRE. Peace Nephew let mee heare no more of e'm, it mads
  mee, thou shalt prevent e'm all, no words to the widdow of my

comming hether, let mee see, tis now upon nine, before twelve Nephew we will have the bargaine struck, wee will ifaith boye.
WITT-GOOD. Oh my pretious Uncle. *Exeunt.*

⟨SCENE II⟩

⟨*Enter*⟩ HOORD *and his* NEECE.

HOORD. Neece, sweete Neece, prethee have a care to my house,
I leave al to thy discretion, be content to dreame a while, ile
have a husband for thee shortly, put that care upon me wench,
for in choosing wives and husbands I am onely fortunate, I have
that gift given me. *Exit.*
NEECE. But tis not likely you should chuse for me,
Since Nephew to your cheifest enimy
Is he whome I affect, but oh forgetfull,
Why dost thou flatter thy affections so
With name of him, that for a widdowes bed,
Neglects thy purer love, can it be so?
Or do's report dissemble:

⟨*Enter* GEORGE.⟩

how now sir?
GEORGE. A letter with which came a private charge.
NEECE. Therein I thanke your care—

⟨*Exit* GEORGE.⟩

I knowe this hand,

Reades

Deerer then sight, what the world reports of me yet beleeve not, rumour will alter shortly, be thou constant, I am still the same that I was in love, and I hope to be the same in fortunes.
Theodorus Wit-good.
I am resolvde, no more shall feare or doubt,
Raise their pale powers to keepe affection out.

Exit.

⟨SCENE III⟩

Enter with a DRAWER, HOORD, *and two* GENTLEMEN.

DRAWER. You're very welcome Gentlemen, Dick showe those Gentlemen the Pomgranite there,—
HOORD. Hist—
DRAWER. Up those staires Gentlemen.
HOORD. Pist Drawer,—
DRAWER. Anon sir?
HOORD. Prethe aske at the Bar, if a gentlewoman came not in lately?
DRAWER. William at the Bar did you see any Gentlewoman come in lately, speake you I, speake you no.
WITHIN. No, none came in yet but mistres Florence.
DRAWER. Hee saies none came in yet sir, but one Mistres Florence.
HOORD. What is that Florence? a widdow!
DRAWER. Yes a duch widdow.
HOORD. How?
DRAWER. Thats an English drab sir, give your worship good morrow.
HOORD. A merry knave ifaith, I shall remember a dutch widdow the longest day of my life.
FIRST GENTLEMAN. Did not I use most art to win the widdow.
SECOND GENTLEMAN. You shall pardon mee for that sir, Maister H*oord* knowes I tooke her at best vantage.
HOORD. What's that sweete Gentlemen, what's that?
SECOND GENTLEMAN. He will needs beare me downe that his art onely, wrought with the widdow most.
HOORD. Oh you did both well Gentlemen, you did both well, I thanke you.
FIRST GENTLEMAN. I was the first that mov'd her.
HOORD. You were ifaith.
SECOND GENTLEMAN. But it was I that tooke her at the bound.
HOORD. I, that was you, faith Gentlemen, tis right.
THIRD GENTLEMAN. I boasted least, but twas I joynd their hands.

Hoord. By'th masse I thinke hee did, you did all well gentlemen, you did al wel, contend no more.
First Gentleman. Come yon roomes fittest.
Hoord. True tis next the doore?

Exit ⟨Hoord *and* Gentlemen.⟩

Enter Witt-good, Curtizan, *and* Host.

Drawer. Your verie welcome, please you to walke up staires cloths layde sir.
Curtizan. Up staires! troth I am weary Maister *Wit-good*.
Witt-good. Rest your selfe here a while widdowe, wee'le have a cup of Muscadine in this little Roome.
Drawer. A cup of Muscadine, you shall have the best sir.
Witt-good. But do you heare sirrah.
Drawer. Do you call, anon sir.
Witt-good. What is there provided for dinner?
Drawer. I cannot readily tell you sir, if you please, you may goe into the kitchin and see your selfe sir, many Gentlemen of worship do use to do it, I assure you sir? ⟨*Exit.*⟩
Host. A prety familiar Priggin raskall, hee has his part with-out booke?
Witt-good. Against you are ready to drinck to mee, widdow, ile bee present to pledge you.
Curtizan. Nay I commend your care, tis donne well of you?

⟨*Exit* Witt-good.⟩

alasse what have I forgot.
Host. What Mistres?
Curtizan. I slipt my wedding Ring off when I washt, and left it at my lodging, prethee run, I shall be sad without it,

⟨*Exit* Host.⟩

so, hee's gon!—boye?

⟨*Enter* Boy.⟩

Boy. Anon forsooth?

III. III. 56. alasse] asse Q1. *In* Q1, *this is the first word in the line, and is indented about two letter-spaces; the* al *probably fell out while the line was being transferred to the chase.* Dyce *amends to* 'Las, *but the* Q1 *spelling is invariably* alasse.

CURTIZAN. Come hether sirrah, learne secretly if one Maister *Hoord* an antient Gentleman be about house?
BOY. I heard such a one nam'd.
CURTIZAN. Commend me to him—

Enter HOORD *with* GENTLEMEN.

HOORD. Ile do thy commendations?
CURTIZAN. Oh you come well: away, to boate, be gon.
HOORD. Thus wisemen are reveng'd give two for one.

Exeunt ⟨HOORD, CURTIZAN, *and* GENTLEMEN.⟩

Enter WITT-GOOD *and* VINTNER.

WITT-GOOD. I must request you sir, to show extraordinary care, my Uncle comes with Gentlemen his friends, and tis upon a making?
VINTNER. Is it so?
Ile give a spetiall charge good Maister *Wit-good*, may I be bold to see her?
WITT-GOOD. Who the widdow?
Withall my heart ifayth, ile bring you to her?
VINTNER. If shee bee a *Staffordsheere* Gentlewoman, tis much if I know her not,—
WITT-GOOD. How now, boy, drawer.
VINTNER. Hie?
BOY. Do you call sir?
WITT-GOOD. Went the Gentlewoman up that was here?
BOY. Up sir? she went out sir.
WITT-GOOD. Out sir?
BOY. Out sir: one Maister *Hoord* with a guard of Gentlemen carried her out at backdoore, a pretie while since sir.
WITT-GOOD. *Hoord*, death and darkenesse, *Hoord*.

Enter HOST.

HOST. The devill of ring I can finde?
WITT-GOOD. How now, what newes, where's the widdow?
HOST. My Mistris? is she not here sir?
WITT-GOOD. More madnes yet.
HOST. Shee sent me for a Ring.

WITT-GOOD. A plot, a plot: to Boate shee's stole away.
HOST. What?

Enter LUCRE *with* GENTLEMEN.

WITT-GOOD. Follow, enquire, old H*oord* my Uncles Adversary— 95
⟨*Exit* HOST.⟩

LUCRE. Nephew, what's that?
WITT-GOOD. Thrice miserable wretch.
LUCRE. Why what's the matter?
VINTNER. The widdow's borne away sir?
LUCRE. Ha, passion of me, a heavy welcome Gentlemen. 100
FIRST GENTLEMAN. The widdow gon?
LUCRE. Who durst attempt it?
WITT-GOOD. Who but old H*oord*, my Uncles adversary?
LUCRE. How?
WITT-GOOD. With his confederates. 105
LUCRE. H*oord*, my deadly enimy, Gentlemen stand to me,
  I will not beare it, 'tis in hate of me,
  That villaine seekes my shame, nay thrists my bloud, hee owes me mortall malice,
  Ile spend my wealth on this despitefull plot, 110
  Ere he shall crosse me and my Nephew thus.
WITT-GOOD. So malitiouslie.

Enter HOST.

LUCRE. How now you treacherous Rascall?
HOST. That's none of my name sir.
WITT-GOOD. Poore soule he knew not on't. 115
LUCRE. Ime sory, I see then 'twas a meere plot.
HOST. I trac'de e'm neerely.—
LUCRE. Well.
HOST. And heare for certaine, they have tooke *Cole-harbor*.
LUCRE. The Divils Sanctuary, 120
  They shall not rest, Ile pluck her from his armes,
  Kind and deere Gentlemen, if ever I had seat within your brests—

  III. III. 108. thrists] thrifts Q1. DYCE *reads* thrists, *which implies inversion of two letters plus foul case; but the substitution of* f *for* s *by foul case is impossible, because* st *was a joined pair, whereas* f *and* t *were separate letters. Probably the ms. read* thrists, *but this was unfamiliar to the compositor, who misread it as* thrifts.

FIRST GENTLEMAN. No more good sir, it is a wrong to us,
  To see you injur'd in a cause so just:
  Weele spend our lives, but we will right our friends.
LUCRE. Honest, and kind, come, we have delayd to long,
  Nephew take comfort; a Just cause is strong.

Exeunt ⟨all except WITT-GOOD⟩.

WITT-GOOD. Thats all my comfort Uncle, ha, ha, ha.
  Now may events fall luckily, and well,
  He that nere strives, sayes wit shall nere excell.

Exit.

⟨SCENE IV⟩

Enter DAMPIT, *the Usurer drunke.*

DAMPIT. When did I say my prayers? In Anno 88. when the great Armado was comming, and In Anno .99. when the great Thundring and Lighting was I prayd heartily then ifaith, to overthrow Poovyes new buildings, I kneeld by my great iron chest I remember.

⟨*Enter* AUDRY.⟩

AUDRY. Maister *Dampit*, one may heare you, before they see you, you keepe sweet howers Maister *Dampit*, we were all a bed 3 howers agoe.
DAMPIT. *Audry.*
AUDRY. Oh yare a fine Gentleman.
DAMPIT. So I am ifaith, and a fine Scholler, do you use to goe to bed, so earely *Audry*?
AUDRY. Call you this earely Maister *Dampit*.
DAMPIT. Why ist not one of Clocke ith morning, is not that earely inough? fetch me a glasse of fresh-Beere.
AUDRY. Here, I have warmd your Nightcap for you maister *Dampit*.
DAMPIT. Draw it on then—I am very weake truely, I have not eaten so much as the bulke of an Egge these 3. dayes.
AUDRY. You have drunke the more Maister *Dampit*.

DAMPIT. Whats that?

AUDRY. You mought, and you would Maister *Dampit*.

DAMPIT. I answer you I cannot, hold your prating, you prate too much, and understand too litle, are you answered,—give me a glasse of beare.

AUDRY. May I aske you how you doe Maister *Dampit*?

DAMPIT. How do I? ifaith naught.

AUDRY. I nere knew you do otherwise.

DAMPIT. I eate not one pennort of bread these 2. yeares, give me a glasse of fresh beere,—I am not sicke, nor I am not well.—

AUDRY. Take this warme Napken about your necke sir, whilst I helpe to make you unready.

DAMPIT. How now *Audrie*-prater, with your skirvy devices, what say you now?

AUDRY. What say I Maister *Dampit*? I say nothing but that you are very weake.

DAMPIT. Faith thou hast more cunnycatching devices then all London?

AUDRY. Why Maister *Dampit* I never deceiv'd you in al my life?

DAMPIT. Why was that? because I never did trust thee.

AUDRY. I care not what you say Maister *Dampit*?

DAMPIT. Hold thy prating, I answere thee, thou art a beggar, a queane, and a bawde: are you answerd.

AUDRY. Fie Maister *Dampit*, a Gentleman and have such words.

DAMPIT. Why thou base drudge of infortunity, thou kitchin-stuffe drab of Beggery, Roguery and cockscombrie, thou Cavernesed queane of foolery, knavery and baudreaminy, ile tell thee what, I will not give a lowse for thy fortunes.

AUDRY. No, maister *Dampit*, and there's a Gentleman comes a wooing to me, and he doubts nothing but that you will get mee from him.

DAMPIT. I, if I would either have thee or lie with thee for two thousand pound, would I might bee dambd, why thou base impudent queane of foolery, flattery, and cockscombry, are you answerd?

AUDRY. Come will you rise and goe to bed sir?

DAMPIT. Rise, and go to bed too *Audry*? how do's Misters Proserpine?

AUDRY. Fooh—

DAMPIT. She's as fine a Philosipher of a stinkards wife, as any 60
within the liberties,—fah, fah *Audry*.
AUDRY. How now Maister *Dampit*?
DAMPIT. Fie upon't, what a choise of stinckes here is, what hast
thou don *Audry*? fie uppon't, here's a choice of stinckes indeed;
give me a glasse of fresh Beere, and then I wil to bed. 65
AUDRY. It waites for you above sir?
DAMPIT. Foh, I thinke they burne hornes in Barnards Inne, if
ever I smelt such an abhominable stinck, usury forsake me.

⟨*Exit.*⟩

AUDRY. They be the stincking nailes of his trampling feete, and he
talkes of burning of hornes. 70
Exit.

ACT IV

⟨SCENE I⟩

Enter at Cole-harbour, HOORD, *the Widdow* ⟨*i.e.*
CURTIZAN⟩ *and Gentlemen* ⟨*including* LAMPREY *and*
SPICHCOCKE⟩, *he married now.*

FIRST GENTLEMAN. Joyne hearts, joyne hands, In wedlocks
bands,
Never to part, till death cleave your heart,
You shall forsake all other women,
You Lords, Knights, Gentlemen, and Yeomen.
What my tongue slips, make up with your lips. 5
HOORD. Give you joy Mistresse H*oord*, let the kisse come about.

⟨*Knocking.*⟩

Who knocks? convay my little Pig-eater out.
LUCRE. ⟨*Within.*⟩ H*oord*?
HOORD. Upon my life, my adversary, Gentlemen.
LUCRE. H*oord*, open the doore, or we will force it ope, 10
Give us the widdow.
HOORD. Gentlemen keepe'm out.

LAMPREY. Hee comes upon his death that enters here.
LUCRE. My friends assist me.
HOORD. Hee has assistants, Gentlemen.
LAMPREY. Tut, nor him, nor them, we in this action feare.
LUCRE. Shall I in peace, speake one word with the widow?
CURTIZAN. Husband and Gentlemen, heare me but a word.
HOORD. Freely sweete wife.
CURTIZAN. Let him in peaceably, you know we're sure, from any act of his.
HOORD. Most true.
CURTIZAN. You may stand by and smile at his old weakenesse, let mee alone to answere him.
HOORD. Content,
Twill be good mirth ifaith, how thinke you Gentlemen?
LAMPREY. Good gullery?
HOORD. Upon calme conditions let him in.
LUCRE. All spite and malice—
LAMPREY. Heare me Maister *Lucre*, so you will vow a peacefull entrance with those your friends and onely exercize
Calme conference with the widdow, without fury,
The passage shall receive you.
LUCRE. I do vow it.
LAMPREY. Then enter and talke freely, here she stands.

Enter LUCRE ⟨GENTLEMEN, *and* HOST⟩.

LUCRE. Oh Maister H*oord*, your spite has wacht the houre, your excellent at vengeance Maister H*oord*.
HOORD. Ha, ha, ha.
LUCRE. I am the foole you laugh at, you are wise sir and knowe the seasons, well, come hether widdow, why is it thus!

⟨LUCRE *and his companions take the* CURTIZAN *aside.*⟩

Oh you have done me infinite disgrace,
And your owne credit no small Injury,
Suffer mine enimy so dispitefully
To beare you from my Nephewe, oh,

IV. I. 23. CURTIZAN.] *Court.* DILKE; *Lu.* Q1.

  I had rather halfe my substance had beene forfet, and begd by
  some starv'd Raskall.
CURTIZAN. Why what would you wish me do sir?
  I must not overthrow my state for love,
  We have too many presidents for that,
  From thousands of our welthie undon widdowes
  One may derive some wit; I do confesse,
  I lov'd your Nephew, nay I did affect him,
  Against the minde and liking of my friend:
  Beleev'd his promises, lay here in hope,
  Of flatterd living, and the boast of lands,
  Comming to touch his wealth and state indeed,
  It appeares drosse, I finde him not the man,
  Imperfect, meane, scarce furnisht of his needes:
  In words, faire Lordships, in performance Hovills,
  Can any woman love the thing that is not?
LUCRE. Broke you for this?
CURTIZAN. Was it not cause too much?
  Send to enquire his state, most part of it,
  Lay two yeares morgag'd in his Uncles hands.
LUCRE. Why say it did, you might have knowne my minde; I
  could have soone restorde it.
CURTIZAN. I, had I but seene any such thing perform'd why
  twould have tyed my affection, and contaynd me in my first
  desires, doe you thinke ifayth, that I could twine such a dry oake
  as this, had promise in your Nephew tooke effect.
LUCRE. Why, and there's no time past, and rather then my
  adversary should thus thw'art my hopes, I would—
CURTIZAN. Tut, y'ave beene ever full of golden speech,
  If wordes were lands, your Nephew would bee rich.
LUCRE. Widdow, beleeve it, I vowe by my best blisse,
  Before these Gentlemen, I will give in
  The morgage to my Nephew instantly,
  Before I sleepe or eate.
FIRST GENTLEMAN. Weele pawne our credits widdow, what he
  speakes shall be performde in fullnesse.
LUCRE. Nay more I will estate him
  In farder blessings; he shall be my heire,

I have no Sonne,
Ile binde my selfe to that condition.
CURTIZAN. When I shall heare this done, I shall soone yeeld, to 85
reasonable tearmes.
LUCRE. In the meane season,
Will you protest before these Gentlemen,
To keepe your selfe, as you are, now at this present.
CURTIZAN. I do protest before these Gentlemen, 90
I will be as cleere then, as I am now.
LUCRE. I do beleeve you, here's your owne honest servant,
Ile take him along with me.
CURTIZAN. I, with all my heart.
LUCRE. He shall see all performde and bring you word. 95
CURTIZAN. Thats all I waite for.
HOORD. What have you finisht Maister *Lucre*? ha, ha, ha, ha!
LUCRE. So, laugh H*oord*, laugh at your poore enimy, do, the
winde may turne you may be laught at too, yes marry may you
sir—ha, ha, ha? 100

Exeunt ⟨LUCRE, *his* GENTLEMEN, *and* HOST⟩.

HOORD. Ha, ha, ha, if every man that swells in malice,
Could be revengd as happily as I:
He would chuse hate, and forsweare amity.
What did he say wife, prethee?
CURTIZAN. Faith spoke to ease his minde,— 105
HOORD. Oh—o—o—
CURTIZAN. You know now, little to any purpose.
HOORD. True, true, true.
CURTIZAN. He would do mountaines now.
HOORD. I, I, I, I. 110
LAMPREY. Y'ave struck him dead Master H*oord*.
SPICHCOCKE. I and his Nephew desperate.
HOORD. I knowte sirs I,
Never did man so crush his enimy?

Exeunt.

⟨SCENE II⟩

Enter LUCRE *with* GENTLEMEN ⟨*and* HOST⟩ *meeting* SAM FREEDOME.

LUCRE. My sonne in lawe,
Sam Freedome? where's my Nephew?
SAM FREEDOME. O man in lamentation father?
LUCRE. How!
SAM FREEDOME. He thumpes his brest like a gallant Dicer that has lost his doublet, and stands in's shirt to do pennance.
LUCRE. Alasse poore gentleman.
SAM FREEDOME. I warrant, you may heare him sigh in a still evening to your house at Hyegate.
LUCRE. I prethe send him in.
SAM FREEDOME. Were it to do a greater matter, I will not stick with you sir, in regard you married my Mother?
⟨*Exit.*⟩

LUCRE. Sweete Gentlemen cheere him up, I will but fetch the morgage, and returne to you instantly. *Exit.*
FIRST GENTLEMAN. Weele do our best sir?—see where he comes,
E'en joylesse and regardlesse of all forme.

⟨*Enter* WITT-GOOD.⟩

SECOND GENTLEMAN. Why how Maister *Wit-good*, fie, you a firme scholler, and an understanding Gentleman, and give your best partes to passion.
FIRST GENTLEMAN. Come fie?
WITT-GOOD. Oh Gentlemen!—
FIRST GENTLEMAN. Sorrow of mee what a sigh was there sir, nine such widdowes are not worth it.
WITT-GOOD. To be borne from me by that lecher H*oord*.
FIRST GENTLEMAN. That vengeance is your Uncles, being done More in despite to him, then wrong to you,
But we bring comfort now,—
WITT-GOOD. I beseech you Gentlemen.

C

SECOND GENTLEMAN. Cheere thy selfe man, there's hope of her ifayth?
WITT-GOOD. To gladsome, to be true.

Enter LUCRE.

LUCRE. Nephew what cheere? alasse poore Gentleman how art thou changd? call thy fresh bloud into thy cheekes agen, shee comes—
WITT-GOOD. Nothing afflicts me so much,
But that it is your Adversary, Uncle,
And meerely plotted in despite of you.
LUCRE. I thats it mads mee, spites mee? ile spend my wealth, e're he shall carry her so, because I know tis onely to spite me, I this is it,—here Nephew, before these kinde Gentlemen I deliver in your morgage, my promise to the widdow, see tis done, be wise, your once more Maister of your owne, the widdow shall perceive now, you are not altogither such a beggar as the world reputes you, you can make shift to bring her to 300. a yeare sir.
FIRST GENTLEMAN. Berlady and thats no toye sir.
LUCRE. A word Nephew?

⟨*Takes* WITT-GOOD *aside.*⟩

FIRST GENTLEMAN. ⟨*To* HOST.⟩ Now you may certifye the widdow?
LUCRE. You must conceive it a right Nephewe now, to doe you good, I am content to do this.
WITT-GOOD. I know it sir?
LUCRE. But your owne conscience can tell I had it deerely ynough of you?
WITT-GOOD. I thats most certaine.
LUCRE. Much money layde out, beside maney a journey to fetch the rent, I hope youle thinke on't Nephew.
WITT-GOOD. I were worse then a beast else ifayth.
LUCRE. Although to blinde the widdow and the world I out of policy doote, yet there's a conscience Nephew.
WITT-GOOD. Heaven forbid else.
LUCRE. When you are full possest,
Tis nothing to returne it.
WITT-GOOD. Alasse a thing quickly done Uncle.
LUCRE. Well sayd,—you know I give it you but in trust.

WITT-GOOD. Pray let me understand you rightly, Uncle, You give it me but in trust.
LUCRE. No.
WITT-GOOD. That is, you trust me with it.
LUCRE. True, true.
WITT-GOOD. ⟨*Aside.*⟩ But if ever I trust you with it agen, would I might bee trust up for my labour.
LUCRE. You can all witnesse Gentlemen, and you sir yeoman?
HOST. My life for yours sir now, I know my Mistrisses minde to well toward your Nephew, let things be in preparation, and ile traine her hether in most excellent fashion.

Exit.

LUCRE. A good old boy,—wife Ginnee?

Enter WIFE.

WIFE. Whats the newes sir?
LUCRE. The wedding daies at hand, prethee sweete wife, expresse thy houswifery, thou'rt a fine Cooke I knowte, thy first husband married thee out of an Aldermans kitchin, go too, he raisde thee for raysing of paste, what, here's none but friends, most of our beginnings must bee winckt at, Gentlemen I envite you all to my Nephewes wedding against Thursday morning.
FIRST GENTLEMAN. Withall our hearts, and wee shall joye to see your enimy so mockt.
LUCRE. He laught at me, gentlemen, ha, ha, ha.

Exeunt ⟨*all but* WITT-GOOD⟩.

WITT-GOOD. Hee has no conscience, faith would laugh at them, they laugh at one another?
Who then can be so cruell, troth, not I,
I rather pitty now, then ought envie,
I do conceive such joye in mine owne happinesse, I have no leysure yet, to laugh at their follies.

    Thou soule of my estate I kisse thee,
    I misse lifes Comfort when I misse thee.
    Oh never will we part agen,
    Untill I leave the Sight of men,
    We'le nere trust conscience of our kin,
    Since Coosenage brings that title in.

⟨*Exit.*⟩

⟨SCENE III⟩

Enter three CREDITORS.

FIRST CREDITOR. Ile wayte these 7. howers but Ile see him caught.
SECOND CREDITOR. Faith so will I.
THIRD CREDITOR. Hang him prodigall, he's stript of the Widdow.
FIRST CREDITOR. A my Troth shees the wiser, she has made the happier choyse, and I wonder of what Stuffe those widdowes hearts are made of, that wil marry unfledgd Boies, before comely thrumb-chind Gentlemen.

Enter a BOY.

BOY. Newes, newes, newes.
FIRST CREDITOR. What boye?
BOY. The Rioter is caught.
FIRST CREDITOR. So, so, so, so, it warmes me at the heart, I love a life to see Dogs upon men; oh here hee comes.

Enter WITT-GOOD *with* SERJANTS.

WITT-GOOD. My last joy was so great it tooke away the sence of all future afflictions, what a day is here orecast? how soone a black tempest rises?
FIRST CREDITOR. Oh wee may speake with you now sir, whats become of your rich widdow, I thinke you may cast your cap at the widdow, may you not sir.
SECOND CREDITOR. He a rich widdow? who a prodigall, a dayly Rioter, and a nightly vomiter, he a widow of account? he a hole ith counter.
WITT-GOOD. You do well my maisters, to tiranzie over misery, to afflect the afflicted, tis a custome you have here amongst you, I would wish you never leave it and I hope youle do as I bid you.
FIRST CREDITOR. Come, come sir, what say you extempore now to your bill of a hundred pound: a sweet debt, for froating your doublets.
SECOND CREDITOR. Here's mine of forty.
THIRD CREDITOR. Here's mine of fifty.

Witt-good. Pray sirs, youle give me Breath.
First Creditor. No sir, wel'e keepe you out of breath still, then we shall be sure you will not run away from us.
Witt-good. Will you but here me speake?
Second Creditor. You shall pardon us for that sir, we know you have too faire a tong of your owne, you over-came us to lately, a shame take you, we are like to loose all that for want of witnesses, wee dealt in policy then, alwaies when we strive to bee most politique we prove most cockscombs, *Non plus ultra*. I perceive by us, were not ordaynde to thrive by wisdome, and therefore wee must be content to be Trades-men.
Witt-good. Give me but reasonable time, and I protest Ile make you ample Satisfaction.
First Creditor. Do you talke of Reasonable time to us?
Witt-good. Tis true, beasts know no reasonable time.
Second Creditor. Wee must have either mony or carcasse.
Witt-good. Alasse what good will my carcasse do you?
Third Creditor. Oh tis a Secret delight we have amongst us, we that are usde to keepe birds in cages, have the heart to keepe men in prison, I warrant you.
Witt-good. ⟨*Aside.*⟩ I perceive I must crave a litle more Ayde from my wits, do but make shift for me this once, and Ile forsweare ever to trouble you in the like fashion hereafter, Ile have better employment for you, and I live. ⟨*To them.*⟩ Youle give me leave my maisters to make Tryall of my friends and raise all meanes I can.
First Creditor. Thats our desires sir.

Enter Host.

Host. Maister *Wit-good*.
Witt-good. Oh art thou come!
Host. May I speake one word with you in private sir?
Witt-good. No by my faith canst thou, I am in hell here and the Devills will not let me Come to thee.
Creditors. Do you call us divvills, you shall find us Puritanes, beare him away, let em talke as they go, we'le not stand to heare 'em, ah sir, am I a devile, I shall thinke the better of my selfe as long as I live, a Devill ifaith.
Exeunt.

⟨SCENE IV⟩

Enter HOORD.

HOORD. What a Sweet blessing hast thou Maister *Hoord* above a multitude, wilt thou never be thankefull? how dost thou thinke to be blest another time? or dost thou count this the full measure of thy hapines? by my troth I thinke thou doest: not only a wife large in possessions, but spatious in content, she's rich, she's yong, she's fayre, she's wise, when I wake I thinke of her lands that revives me, when I go to bed, I dreame of her beauty, and thats ynough for me, she's worth 4. hundred a yeare in her very smock, if a man knewe how to use it, but the journey will bee all in troth into the Country, to ride to her Lands in state and order following my Brother and other worshipfull Gentlemen whose companies I ha sent downe for already, to ride along with us, in their goodly *Decorum*-beards, their broad Velvet chashocks, and chaines of gold twice or thrice double; against which time, ile entertaine some ten men of mine own, into Liveries, all of occupations or qualities, I will not keepe an idle man about mee, the sight of which will so vexe my Adversary *Lucre*, for weele passe by his dore of purpose, make a little stand for nonce, and have our horses Curvet before the window, certainly he will never endure it, but run up and hang himself presently?

⟨*Enter a* SERVANT.⟩

how now sirra? what newes? any that offer their service to me yet?
SERVANT. Yes sir, there are some ith hall, that waite for your worships liking, and desire to be entertainde.
HOORD. Are they of occupation?
SERVANT. They are men fit for your worship sir.
HOORD. Sayst so? send e'm all in!—⟨*Exit* SERVANT.⟩ to see ten men ride after mee in watchet liveries with Orenge-tawny capes, twill cut his combe ifayth,

IV. IV. 6. wise] Q2; wife Q1.

Enter ⟨Taylor, Barber, Perfumer, Fawlkner, *and* Huntsman⟩.

how now? of what occupation are you sir.
Taylor. A Taylor, an't please your worship.
Hoord. A taylor, oh very good, you shall serve to make all the Liveries—what are you sir?
Barber. A Barber sir.
Hoord. A Barber very needefull, you shall shave all the house, and if neede require stand for a Reaper ith Sommer time,—You sir?
Perfumer. A Perfumer?
Hoord. I smelt you before, Perfumers of all men had neede carry themselves uprightly, for if they were once knaves they would be smelt out quickly,—to you sir?
Fawlkner. A Fawlkner an't please your worship—
Hoord. Sa ho, sa ho, sa ho—and you sir?
Huntsman. A Huntsman sir.
Hoord. There boy, there boye, there boye? I am not so old but I have pleasant daies to come, I promise you my Maisters I take such a good liking to you, that I entertaine you all, I put you already into my countenance, and you shall be shortly in my liverie? but especially you two my jolly Fawlkner, and my bonny huntsman, wee shall have most neede of you at my wifes Mannor-houses ith Country, there's goodly parkes and Champion-grounds for you, we shall have all our sports within our selves, all the Gentlemen ath Country shall bee beholding to us and our pastimes.
Fawlkner. And weele make your worship admire sir.
Hoord. Sayst thou so? doe but make mee admire, and thou shalt want for nothing,—my Taylor?
Taylor. Anon sir.
Hoord. Go presently in hand with the liveries.
Taylor. I will sir.
Hoord. My Barber.
Barber. Here sir.
Hoord. Make e'm all trim fellowes, lowse e'm well, especially my huntsman, and cut all their beards of the Polonian fashion: my perfumer—
Perfumer. Under your nose sir.

Hoord. Cast a better savour upon the knaves, to take away the sent of my Taylors feete, and my Barbers Lotium-water.
Perfumer. It shall be carefully performde sir.
Hoord. But you my Faulkner and Huntsman, the welcomst men alive ifayth.
Huntsman. And weele show you that sir, shall deserve your worshippes favour?
Hoord. I prethee show mee that: goe you knaves all, and wash your lungs ith Buttery, go—

⟨*Exeunt* Taylor, Barber, Perfumer, Fawlkner, *and* Huntsman.⟩

byth masse, and well remembred, ile aske my wife that question, wife, Mistris *Jane Hoord*!

Enter Curtizan *alterd in Apparell.*

Curtizan. Sir? would you with me?
Hoord. I would but know sweet wife, which might stand best to thy liking, to have the wedding dinner kept here or ith Country?
Curtizan. Hum? faith sir twould like me better here, here you were married, here let all rites be ended.
Hoord. Could a Marquesse give a better answere? H*oord* beare thy head aloft, thou'st a wife will advance it,

⟨*Enter* Host, *who gives a letter to* Curtizan.⟩

what haste comes here now? yee a letter: some dregge of my Adversaries malice: come hether, whats the newes!
Host. A thing that concernes my Mistris sir.
Hoord. Why then it concernes me knave?
Host. I and you knave too, (cry your worshippe mercy) you are both like to come into trouble I promise you sir, a præcontract.
Hoord. How a præcontract sayst thou?
Host. I feare they have too much proofe on't sir, old *Lucre* he runs mad up and downe and will to lawe as fast as he can, yong *Witgood* layde hold on by his creditors, hee exclaymes upon you a tother side, saies you have wrought his undoing, by the injurious detayning of his contract.
Hoord. Body a me?

Host. He will have utmost satisfaction.
　The lawe shall give him recompence he saies.
Curtizan. ⟨*Aside.*⟩ Alasse his creditors so mercilesse, my state
　beeing yet uncertaine, I deeme it not unconscionable to furder
　him.
Host. True sir—
Hoord. Wife, what saies that letter, let me construe it.
Curtizan. Curst be my rash and unadvised words,
　Ile set my foote upon my tongue,
　And tread my inconsiderate grant to dust.

⟨*Tears letter and treads on it.*⟩

Hoord. Wife—
Host. ⟨*Aside.*⟩ A prety shift yfaith, I commend a woman when
　shee can make away a letter from her husband handsomely, and
　this was cleanely done by my troth.
Curtizan. I did sir?
　Some foolish words I must confesse did passe,
　Which, now letigiously he fastens on me.
Hoord. Of what force? let me examine e'm.
Curtizan. Too strong I feare, would I were well free'd of him.
Hoord. Shall I compound?
Curtizan. No sir, ide have it done some Nobler way
　Of your side; ide have you come off with honor,
　Let basenesse keepe with them; why have you not the meanes
　sir, the occasions offerd you.
Hoord. Where? how? deere wife.
Curtizan. Hee is now caught by his creditors, the slave's needie,
　his debts petty, hee'le rather binde himselfe, to all inconveniences
　then rot in pryson, by this onely meanes you may get a release
　from him, 'tis not yet come to his Uncles hearing, send speedily
　for the creditors, by this time hee's disperate, hee'le set his hand
　to any thing, take order for his debts, or discharge e'm quite, a
　pax on him, lets be rid of a raskall.
Hoord. Excellent, thou dost astonish mee, go, runne, make hast,
　bring both the creditors and W*it-good* hether.
Host. ⟨*Aside.*⟩ This will be some revenge yet.　⟨*Exit.*⟩
Hoord. In the meane space Ile have a release drawne—within
　there.

⟨*Enter* SERVANT.⟩

SERVANT. Sir.
HOORD. Sirrah, come take directions, goe to my Scrivener.
CURTIZAN. ⟨*Aside.*⟩ Ime yet like those, whose riches lie in dreames,
If I be wakte the're false, such is my fate,
Who ventures deeper then the desperate state.
Though I have sind yet could I become new,
For where I once vow, I am ever true.
HOORD. Away, Dispatch, on my Displeasure, quickly,

⟨*Exit* SERVANT.⟩

happy occasion, pray heaven hee bee in the right Vayne now to set his hand toot, that nothing alter him; grant that al his follyes may meete in him at once, to besot him inough.

⟨*Enter* WITT-GOOD *and the three* CREDITORS.⟩

I pray for him ifaith, and here he comes.
WITT-GOOD. What would you with me now, my Uncles spitefull adversary.
HOORD. Nay I am friends.
WITT-GOOD. I when your mischeifes spent.
HOORD. I heard you were arrested.
WITT-GOOD. Wel, what then? you wil pay none of my debts I am sure.
HOORD. A wiseman cannot tell,
There may be those Conditions greed upon,
May move me to do much.
WITT-GOOD. I when? Tis thou perjured Woman, O no name
Is vild inough to match thy trechery,
That art the cause of my confusion.
CURTIZAN. Out you penurious slave.
HOORD. Nay wife you are too froward,
Let him alone, give loosers leave to talke.
WITT-GOOD. Shall I remember thee of an other promise far stronger then the first.
CURTIZAN. Ide faine knowe that.

WITT-GOOD. Twould call shame to thy cheeks.
CURTIZAN. Shame.
WITT-GOOD. Harke in your ear.—
⟨*Takes her aside.*⟩

Will hee come of thinkst thou, and pay my Debts roundly?
CURTIZAN. Doubt nothing, theres a Release a drawing and all to which you must set your hand.
WITT-GOOD. Excellent.
CURTIZAN. But mee thinkes ifaith you might have made some shift to discharge this your selfe, having in the morgage, and never have burdned my conscience with it.
WITT-GOOD. A my troth I could not, for my creditors cruelties extend to the present.
CURTIZAN. No more,—⟨*Aloud.*⟩ why do your worst for that, I defie you.
WITT-GOOD. Y'are impudent, ile call up witnesses.
CURTIZAN. Call up thy wits for thou hast beene devoted to follies a long time.
HOORD. Wife, y'are too bitter? Maister *Wit-good*, and you my Maisters, you shal heare a milde speech come from me now, and this it is, tas beene my fortune, Gentlemen, to have an extraordinary blessing powr'd upon me alate, and here she stands, I have wedded her and bedded her, and yet she is little the worse, some foolish wordes shee hath past to you in the Country, and some peevish debts you owe here in the Citty, set the Hares head to the Goose-giblet, release you her of her words, and ile release you of your debts sir.
WITT-GOOD. Would you so, I thanke you for that sir, I cannot blame you ifayth.
HOORD. Why are not debts better then words sir?
WITT-GOOD. Are not words promises, and are not promises debts sir.
HOORD. He plaies at back-Racket with me.
FIRST CREDITOR. Come hether Maister *Wit-good* come hether, be rulde by fooles once.
SECOND CREDITOR. We are Cittizens and know what belong toote.

FIRST CREDITOR. Take hold of his offer, pax on her, let her goe, if your debts were once discharg'd, I would helpe you to a widdow my selfe worth ten of her.
THIRD CREDITOR. Masse partner and now you remember mee on't, there's Maister Muligrubs sister newly falne a widdow.
FIRST CREDITOR. Cuds mee, as pat as can be, there's a widdow left for you, ten thousand in mony, beside Plate, Jewells *et cætera*, I warrant it a match, wee can do all in all with her, prethee dispatch weele carry thee to her presently.
WITT-GOOD. My Uncle will nere endure me, when he shall heare I set my hand to a release.
SECOND CREDITOR. Harke, ile tell thee a *Trick* for that, I have spent five hundred pound in suites in my time, I should be wise, thou'rt now a prisoner, make a release, takte of my worde, whatsoever a man makes as long as he is in durance, tis nothing in lawe, not thus much.

⟨*Snaps his fingers.*⟩

WITT-GOOD. Say you so sir?
THIRD CREDITOR. I have payde for't I know't.
WITT-GOOD. Proceede then, I consent.
THIRD CREDITOR. Why wel sayde.
HOORD. How now my Maisters, what have you done with him?
FIRST CREDITOR. With much a doe sir, we have got him to consent.
HOORD. Ah—a—a,—and what came his debts to now?
FIRST CREDITOR. Some eight score od pounds sir.
HOORD. Nau, nau, nau, nau, naw, tell me the second time, give me a lighter somme, they are but desperate debts you know, neere cald in but upon such an accident, a poore needy knave hee would starve and rot in prison, come, come, you shall have ten shillings in the pound and the somme downe roundly—
FIRST CREDITOR. You must make it a marke sir,—
HOORD. Go too then, tell your mony in the meane time, you shall finde little lesse there,—

⟨*Gives them money.*⟩

come Maister *Wit-good* you are so unwilling to do your selfe good now,

⟨*Enter a* SCRIVENER.⟩

welcome honest Scrivener, now you shall heare the release read,—

⟨*The* SCRIVENER *reads*.⟩

SCRIVENER. Be it known, to al men by these presents, that I *Theodorus Wit-good*, Gentleman, sole Nephew to *Pecunious Lucre*, having unjustly made title and claime, to one *Jane Medler*, late widdow of *Anthony Medler*, and now wife to *Walkadine Hoord*, in consideration of a competent som of mony to discharge my debts, do for ever hereafter disclaime any title, right, estate, or interest in or to the sayd widdow late in the occupation of the sayd *Anthony Medler*, and now in the occupation of *Walkadine Hoord*, as also neither to laye claime, by vertue of any former contract, grant, promise or demise, to any of her Mannor, Mannorhouses, Parkes, Groves, Meadow-grounds, arrable lands, Barnes, stacks, Stables, Dove-holes, and Cunny-borrowes; togither with al her cattell, money, plate, jewells, borders, chaines, bracelets, furnitures, hangings, move-ables, or immoveables, in wittnesse wher-of I the sayd *Theodorus Wit-good*, have enterchangeably set to my hand and seale before these presents, the daie, and date above written.

WITT-GOOD. What a pretious fortune hast thou slipt here like a beast as thou art?

HOORD. Come, unwilling heart come.

WITT-GOOD. Well Maister *Hoord*, give me the pen, I see Tis vaine to quarrell with our destiny.

HOORD. Oh as vaine a thing as can bee, you cannot commit a greater absurdity sir,—

⟨WITT-GOOD *signs the release.*⟩

so, so, give mee that hand now, before al these presents I am friends for ever with thee.

WITT-GOOD. Troth, and it were pitty of my heart now, if I should beare you any grudge yfaith.

HOORD. Content, ile send for thy Uncle against the wedding dinner, we will be friends once agen.

WITT-GOOD. I hope to bring it to passe my selfe sir?

HOORD. How now? ist right my masters?

FIRST CREDITOR. Tis somthing wanting sir, yet it shall be sufficient.

HOORD. Why well sayd, a good conscience makes a fine showe now a daies, come my Maisters you shall all tast of my wine ere you depart.

ALL. We follow you sir?

⟨*Exeunt* HOORD, CURTIZAN, *and* SCRIVENER.⟩

WITT-GOOD. ⟨*Aside.*⟩ Ile try these fellowes now,— a word sir, what will you carry me to that widdow now?

FIRST CREDITOR. Why do you thinke we were in earnest yfaith? carry you to a rich widdow, wee should get much credit by that; a noted Rioter, a contemptible prodigall, twas a T*r*ick we have amongst us, to get in our mony, fare you well sir.

Exeunt ⟨CREDITORS⟩.

WITT-GOOD. Farewell and be hangd, you short-pig-hayrde Ram-headed raskalls, he that beleeves in you, shall nere be sav'd I warrant him, by this new league, I shall have some accesse unto my love—

She ⟨*i.e. the* NEECE⟩ *is above.*

NEECE. Maister W*i*t-*good*?

WITT-GOOD. My life.

NEECE. Meete me presently, that note directs you,

⟨*She throws a letter down to him.*⟩

I would not be suspected, our happinesse attends us, farewell?

WITT-GOOD. A words ynough. *Exeunt.*

⟨SCENE V⟩

DAMPIT *the Usurer in his bed,* AUDRY *spinning by* ⟨*and* BOY *serving drink*⟩.

Song. Let the Usurer cram him, in interest that excell,
       There's pits enow to dam him, before he comes to hell.
       In Holborne, some: in Fleete-street some,
       Where ere he come, there's some there's some.

DAMPIT. *Trahe, traheto,* drawe the Curtaine, give mee a sippe of
Sack more.

Enter GENTLEMEN ⟨*including* LAMPREY *and* SPICHCOCKE⟩.

LAMPREY. Looke you, did not I tell you he lay like the devill in
chaines, when he was bound for a thousand yeare.
SPICHCOCKE. But I thinke the devill had no steele Bedstaffes, he
goes beyond him for that.
LAMPREY. Nay doe but marke the conceite of his drincking, one
must wipe his mouth for him with a muckinder, do you see sir.
SPICHCOCKE. Is this the sick trampler, why he is onely bed-red
with drinking.
LAMPREY. True sir, he spies us.
DAMPIT. What? sir Tristram? you come and see a weake man here,
a very weake man,—
LAMPREY. If you be weake in body, you should be strong in
prayer sir.
DAMPIT. Oh, I have pray'd too much poore man.
LAMPREY. There's a tast of his soule for you.
SPICHCOCKE. Fah, loathsome?
LAMPREY. I come to borrow a hundred pound of you sir.
DAMPIT. Alasse you come at an ill time, I cannot spare it ifayth,
I ha but two thousand ith house.
AUDRY. Ha, ha, ha.
DAMPIT. Out you gernative queane, the mullipoop of villany,
the Spinner of concupiscency.

Enter other GENTLEMEN ⟨*including* SIR LANCELOT⟩.

SIR LANCELOT. Yee gentlemen are you here before us? how is
hee now?
LAMPREY. Faith the same man still, the Taverne bitch has bit him
ith head.
SIR LANCELOT. Wee shall have the better sport with him, peace,
and how cheeres Maister *Dampit* now?
DAMPIT. Oh, my bosome sir *Lancelot,* how cheere I? thy presence
is restorative.
SIR LANCELOT. But I heare a great complaint of you Maister
Dampit, among gallants.
DAMPIT. I am glad of that ifayth;—prethee what?

Sir Lancelot. They say you are waxte proud alate, and if a friend visit you in the after-noone, you'le scarce know him.

Dampit. Fie, fie, proud? I cannot remember any such thing, sure I was drunck then.

Sir Lancelot. Thinke you so sir?

Dampit. There twas ifayth, nothing but the pride of the Sack and so certifie e'm, fetch Sack sirrah.

Boy. ⟨*Aside.*⟩ A vengeance Sack you once.

Audry. Why Maister *Dampit* if you hold on as you begin, and lie a little longer, you neede not take care how to dispose your wealth, you'le make the Vintner your heire.

Dampit. Out you babliaminy, you unfetherd cremitoryed queane, you cullisance of scabiosity.

Audry. Good words Maister *Dampit*, to speake before a maide and a virgin.

Dampit. Hang thy virginity, upon the pole of carnality.

Audry. Sweete tearmes, my Mistris shall know e'm.

Lamprey. Note but the misery of this usuring slave, here hee lies like a noysome dunghill, full of the poyson of his druncken blasphemies, and they to whome he bequeathes all, grudge him the very meate that feedes him, the very pillow that eases him, here may a usurer behold his end, what profits it to be a slave in this world, and a devil ith next.

Dampit. Sir L*ancelot*? let me busse thee sir *Lancelot*, thou art the onely friend that I honor and respect.

Sir Lancelot. I thanke you for that Maister D*ampit*.

Dampit. Farewell my bosome sir *Lancelot*.

Sir Lancelot. Gentlemen, and you love mee, let mee step behinde you, and one of you fall a talking of me to him.

Lamprey. Content—Maister D*ampit*.

Dampit. So sir.

Lamprey. Here came sir *Lancelot* to see you e'en now.

Dampit. Hang him raskall.

Lamprey. Who sir *Lancelot*?

Dampit. Pythagoricall raskall.

Lamprey. Pythagoricall?

Dampit. I he changes his cloake when he meetes a Sergiant.

Sir Lancelot. What a rogues this?

LAMPREY. I wonder you can raile at him sir, he comes in love to see you.
DAMPIT. A louse for his love, his father was a Combe-maker, I have no neede of his crawling love, hee comes to have longer day, the superlative raskall.
SIR LANCELOT. Sfoote I can no longer endure the rogue, Maister D*ampit*, I come to take my leave once agen sir?
DAMPIT. Who? my deere and kinde Sir *Lancelot*? the onely Gentleman of England, let me hug thee, farewell and a thousand.
LAMPREY. Composde of wrongs and slavish flatteries.
SIR LANCELOT. Nay Gentlemen, he shall show you more *Tricks* yet, ile give you another tast of him.
LAMPREY. I'st possible?
SIR LANCELOT. His memory is upon departing.
DAMPIT. Another cup of Sack.
SIR LANCELOT. Masse then twill be quite gon: before he drinke that, tell him theres a cuntry client come up, and here attends for his Learned advice.
LAMPREY. Inough.
DAMPIT. One Cup more, and then let the Bell toale, I hope I shall be weake inough by that time.
LAMPREY. Maister *Dampit*.
DAMPIT. Is the Sack spouting?
LAMPREY. Tis comming forward sir,—heres a countryman a client of yours, waytes for your deepe and profound advice sir.
DAMPIT. A cockscombry? where is he? let him approch, set me up a pegge higher.
LAMPREY. You must draw nere sir.
DAMPIT. Now good-man fooleaminy, what say you to me now?
SIR LANCELOT. Please your good worship, I am a poore man sir—
DAMPIT. What make you in my Chamber then?
SIR LANCELOT. I would entreate your worships device in a just and honest cause sir—
DAMPIT. I meddle with no such matters, I refer e'm, to Maister No-mans Office.
SIR LANCELOT. I had but one house left me in all the world sir which was my fathers, my Grand-fathers, my great Grandfathers,

and now a Villaine has unjustly wrung me out, and tooke possession ont.

DAMPIT. Has he such feates? thy best course is to bring thy *ejectione firme*, and in Seaven yeare thou mayst shove him out by the Law.

SIR LANCELOT. Alasse, ant please your worship, I have small friends and lesse mony.

DAMPIT. Hoyda, this geere will fadge well, hast no money, why then my advice is thou must set fire ath house and so get him out.

LAMPREY. That will breake strife indeed.

SIR LANCELOT. I thanke your worship for your hot Counsell sir.—Altring but my voyce alitle, you see he knew me not, you may observe by this that a drunkards memory, holds longer in the voyce then in the person, but Gentlemen shall I show you a sight, behold the litle dive-dapper of Damnation, *Gulfe* the usurer, for his time worse then tother.

Enter HOORD *with* GULFE.

LAMPREY. What's he comes with him?

SIR LANCELOT. Why H*oord*, that maried lately the widdowe Medler.

LAMPREY. Oh, I cry you mercy sir.

HOORD. Now gentlemen visitants? how dos maister *Dampit*?

SIR LANCELOT. Faith here hee lies e'n drawing—in sir, good canary as fast as hee can sir, a very weake creature truely, hee is almost past memory.

HOORD. Fie Maister *Dampit*: you lie lazing a bed here, and I come to envite you to my wedding dinner, up, up, up.

DAMPIT. Whose this maister H*oord*! who hast thou married in the name of foolery.

HOORD. A rich widdow.

DAMPIT. A Duch widdow.

HOORD. A ritch widdow,—one widdow Medler.

DAMPIT. Medler she keepes open house.

HOORD. She did I can tell you in her tother husbands dayes, open house for all comers, horse and man was welcome, and Roome inough for em all.

DAMPIT. Theres to much for thee then, thou mayst let out some to thy Neighbours.

GULFE. What? hung a live in chaynes? O Spectacle, bedstaffs of steele, *O monstrum, horrendum, Informe, Ingens cui Lumen ademptum*, O *Dampit, Dampit*, heres a Just judgment, showne upon usury, extortion, and trampling Villany.
SIR LANCELOT. ⟨*Aside.*⟩ This exlent, theefe rayles upon the Theefe.
GULFE. Is this the end of cut throate Usury, Brothell, and blasphemy? now maist thou see what Race a Usurer runnes.
DAMPIT. Why thou Rogue of universality, do not I know thee? thy Sound is like the cuckowe, the welch Embassador, thou cowardly slave that offers to fight with a sicke man when his weapons downe: rayle upon me in my naked bed? why thou great Lucifers litle vicar, I am not so weake but I know a knave at first sight, thou Inconscionable Raskall, thou that goest upon middlesex Juryes, and will make hast to give up thy verdit, because thou wilt not loose thy dinner, are you answered?
GULFE. Ant twere not for shame—

Drawes his dagger.

DAMPIT. Thou wouldst be hangd then.
LAMPREY. Nay you must exercize patience Maister *Gulfe*, alwayes in a sick-mans Chamber.
SIR LANCELOT. 'Heele quarrell with none I warrant you, but those that are bedred.
DAMPIT. Let him come Gentlemen, I am arm'd, reach my closse stoole hether.
SIR LANCELOT. Here wilbe a sweet fraie anon, Ile leave you gentlemen.
LAMPREY. Nay wel'e a long with you, Maister *Gulfe*—
GULFE. Hang him usuring raskall.
SIR LANCELOT. Push, set your Strenght to his, your wit to his.
AUDRY. Pray Gentlemen depart, his howers come upon him, sleepe in my bosome, sleepe.
SIR LANCELOT. Nay we have inough of him ifaith, keepe him for the house.—Now make your best.
For thrice his wealth, I would not have his brest.
GULFE. A litle thing would make me beat him, now he's asleep.

IV. v. 180. *Gulfe*—] Gulf— DYCE; *Gulfe.* Q1.

Sir Lancelot. Masse then twilbe a pittifull day when he wakes.

I would be loath to see that day, come.

Gulfe. You over-rule me gentlemen ifaith.

Exeunt.

ACT V

⟨SCENE I⟩

Enter Lucre *and* Witt-good.

Witt-good. Nay uncle, let me prevayle with you so much, Ifaith go, now he has envited you.

Lucre. I shall have great joy there, when he has borne away the widdow.

Witt-good. Why la, I thought where I should find you presently; Uncle, a my troth, tis nothing so.

Lucre. Whats nothing so sir, is not he maried to the widdow.

Witt-good. No by my troth is he not Uncle.

Lucre. How?

Witt-good. Will you have the truth ont, he is married to a whore ifaith.

Lucre. I should laugh at that.

Witt-good. Uncle, let me perish in your favour if you find it not so and that tis I that have married the honest woman.

Lucre. Ha? Ide walke ten mile a foot to see that ifaith.

Witt-good. And see'te you shall, or Ile nere see you agen.

Lucre. A Queane ifaith? ha, ha, ha.

Exeunt.

⟨SCENE II⟩

Enter Hoord *tasting wine the* Host *following in a Livery cloake.*

Hoord. Pup, pup, pup, pup, I like not this wine, is there never a better Teirs in the house?

Host. Yes sir, there are as good Teirs in the house, as any are in England.
Hoord. Desire your mistris you knave, to tast e'm all over, shee has better Skill.
Host. Has she so, the better for her, and the worse for you.

Exit.

Hoord. *Arthur*, is the cupbard of plate set out?

⟨*Enter* Arthur.⟩

Arthur. Al's in order sir. ⟨*Exit.*⟩
Hoord. I am in love with my Liveryes every time I thinke on e'm, they make a gallant show by my troth.—Neece.

⟨*Enter* Neece.⟩

Neece. Do you call sir?
Hoord. Prethee show a litle diligence, and over-looke the knaves a litle, theile filch and steale to day and send whole pasties home to their wives, and thou bee'st a good Neece, do not see me purloynd.
Neece. ⟨*To him.*⟩ Feare it not sir, ⟨*Aside.*⟩ I have cause, tho the feast bee prepared for you, yet it serves fit for my wedding dinner too.

Enter two gentlemen ⟨Lamprey *and* Spichcocke⟩.

Hoord. Maister *Lamprey*, and Maister *Spichcocke* two the most welcome gentlemen alive, your fathers and mine were all free ath Fishmongers.
Lamprey. They were indeed sir, you see bould guestes sir, soone intreated.
Hoord. And thats best sir—

⟨*Enter a* Servant.⟩

how now sirrah?
Servant. Ther's a coach come to'th doore sir. ⟨*Exit.*⟩
Hoord. My Ladie *Foxestone* a my life. Mistris *Jane Hoord*, wife,

⟨*Enter* Ladie Foxestone.⟩

masse tis her Ladyship indeed, Madame you are welcome to an unfurnisht house, dearth of cheere, scarcsity of attendance.

LADIE FOXESTONE. You are pleasd to make the worst sir.

⟨*Enter* CURTIZAN.⟩

HOORD. Wife.
LADIE FOXESTONE. Is this your Bride?
HOORD. Yes Maddam, salute my Lady *Foxtone*.
CURTIZAN. Please you Madam a while to tast the ayre in the garden?
LADIE FOXESTONE. Twill please us well.

Exeunt ⟨CURTIZAN *and* LADIE FOXESTONE.⟩

HOORD. Who would not wed; the most delitious life,
No Joyes are like the comforts of a wife.
LAMPREY. So we bachilers thinke that are not troubled with them.

⟨*Enter a* SERVANT.⟩

SERVANT. Your worships brother with an other antient Gentleman, are newly allighted Sir.

⟨*Enter* ONESIPHORUS HOORD, LIMBER, *and* KIXE.⟩

HOORD. Maister *Onesiphorus Hoord*, why now our company begins to come in: my deere and kind brother welcome ifaith.
ONESIPHORUS HOORD. You see we are men at an hower brother.
HOORD. I, Ile say that for you brother, you keepe as good an hower to come to a feast, as any Gentleman in the Sheere. What ould Maister *Limber* and Maister *Kicks*, doe wee meete ifaith Jolly Gentlemen?
LIMBER. We hope you lack guesse sir?
HOORD. Oh welcome, welcome, wee lack still such guesse as your worships.
ONESIPHORUS HOORD. Ah sirrah brother, have you catcht up widdow Medler.
HOORD. From e'm all brother, and I may tell you, I had mighty enemies, those that stuck sore, old *Lucre* is a sore foxe I can tell you brother.
ONESIPHORUS HOORD. Where is she, ile go seeke her out, I long to have a smack at her lips.

⟨*Enter* Curtizan.⟩

Hoord. And most wishfully brother see where she comes, give her a smerck now we may heare it all the house over.
Curtizan. ⟨*Aside.*⟩ Oh heaven, I am betrayde, I know that face.

Both turne back.

Hoord. Ha, ha, ha, why how now? are you both a shamde? come Gentlemen, weele looke another way—
Onesiphorus Hoord. Nay Brother, harke you, come y'are disposde to be merrie?
Hoord. Why do we meete else man?
Onesiphorus Hoord. That's another matter, I was nere so fread in my life but that you had beene in earnest.
Hoord. How meane you brother?
Onesiphorus Hoord. You sayd she was your wife?
Hoord. Did I so? by my troth and so she is.
Onesiphorus Hoord. By your troth Brother?
Hoord. What reason have I to dissemble with my friends, brother, if marriage can make her mine, she is mine? why?
Onesiphorus Hoord. Troth I am not well of a suddaine? I must crave pardon brother, I came to see you, but I cannot stay dinner yfaith.
Hoord. I hope you will not serve mee so brother.
Limber. By your leave Maister Hoord.
Hoord. What now? what now? pray Gentlemen, you were wont to show your selves wisemen.
Limber. But you have showne your folly too much here.
Hoord. How?
Kixe. Fie, fie, a man of your repute and name,
Youle feast your friends but cloye e'm first with shame.
Hoord. This growes too deepe, pray let us reach the sence.
Limber. In your old age doate on a Curtizan—
Hoord. Ha?
Kixe. Marry a Strumpet?
Hoord. Gentlemen!
Onesiphorus Hoord. And *Wit-goods* queane.
Hoord. Oh, nor Lands, nor living?
Onesiphorus Hoord. Living?

HOORD. Speake?
CURTIZAN. Alasse you know at first sir,
  I told you I had nothing.
HOORD. Out, out, I am cheated, infinitely couzned.
LIMBER. Nay Master H*oord*—

Enter WITT-GOOD *and* LUCRE.

HOORD. A dutch widdow, a dutch widdow, a dutch widdow.
LUCRE. Why Nephew shall I trace thee still a lier? wilt make mee mad, is not yon thing the widdow.
WITT-GOOD. Why la, you are so hard a beleefe Uncle, by my troth she's a whore.
LUCRE. Then thou'rt a knave.
WITT-GOOD. *Negatur Argumentum* Uncle.
LUCRE. *Probo tibi*, Nephew: Hee that knowes a woman to bee a queane must needes bee a knave, thou sayst thou knowst her to bee one, *ergo* if shee bee a queane thou'rt a knave.
WITT-GOOD. *Negatur, sequela majoris*, Uncle, hee that knowes a woman to be a queane must needes be a knave, I deny that.
HOORD. L*ucre*, and W*it-good*, y'are both villaines, get you out of my house.
LUCRE. Why didst not invite me to thy wedding dinner?
WITT-GOOD. And are not you and I sworne perpetuall friends before wittnesse sir, and were both drunck upon't.
HOORD. Daintily abusde, y'ave put a Junt upon me.
LUCRE. Ha, ha, ha.
HOORD. A common strumpet?
WITT-GOOD. Nay now you wrong her sir, if I were shee ide have the lawe on you for that, I durst depose for her, shee nere had common use, nor common thought.
CURTIZAN. Despise me, publish me, I am your wife,
  What shame can I have now but youle have part,
  If in disgrace you share, I sought not you:
  You pursued me, nay forc'st me,
  Had I friends would follow it,
  Lesse then your action has beene prov'd a rape.
ONESIPHORUS HOORD. Brother?
CURTIZAN. Nor did I ever boast of lands unto you,
  Money or goods: I tooke a playner course:

And told you true ide nothing,
If error were committed twas by you. 135
Thanke your owne folly, nor has my sinne beene so odious but worse has bin forgiven, nor am I so deformd but I may challing the utmost power of any old mans love, shee that tasts not sin before, twenty to one but sheele tast it after: most of you ould men are content to mary yong Virgins and take that which 140 followes, where marrying one of us, you both save a sinner, and are quit from a cuckold for ever,
"And more in breife let this your best thoughts winne,
"She that knowes sinne, knowes best how to hate sinne.

HOORD. Curst be all Malice, blacke are the fruites of spite, 145
And poyson first their owners: O my friends,
I must imbrace shame, to be rid of shame,
Conceald disgrace prevents a publick name.
Ah *Wit-good*, ah *Theodorus*.

WITT-GOOD. Alasse sir, I was prickt in conscience to see her 150 well bestowd, and where could I bestowe her beter then upon your pittiful worship: excepting but my selfe, I dare sweare shees a Virgin, and now by marrying your Neece I have banisht my selfe for ever from her, she's mine Aunt now by my faith, and theres no Medling with mine Aunt you know, a sinne against my 155 Nuncle.

CURTIZAN. Lo, Gentlemen, before you all,
In true reclaymed forme I fall,
Hence-forth for ever I defie,
The Glances of a sinnefull eye, 160
Waving of Fans, which some suppose,
Tricks of Fancy, Treading of Toes,
Wringing of Fingers, byting the Lip,
The wanton gate th'alluring Trip,
All secret friends and private meetings, 165
Close borne letters, and Baudes greetings,
Fayning excuse to weomens Labours,
When we are sent for to'th next Neighbours,
Taking false Phisicke, and nere start,
To be let blood, tho signe be at heart, 170
Removing chambers, shifting beds,
To welcome Frends in husbands steads,

  Them to enjoy, and you to marry,
  They first servd, while you must tarry,
  They to spend and you to gather,   175
  They to get and you to father,
  These and thousand thousand more,
  New reclaymed I now abhore.
LUCRE. A, heres a lesson Rioter for you.
WITT-GOOD. I must confesse my follyes, Ile downe to 180
  And Here for ever I disclaime,
  The cause of youths undooing. Game:
  Cheifly dice, those true outlanders,
  That shake out Beggars, Theeves and Panders,
  Soule wasting Surfets, sinfull Riotts,   185
  Queanes Evills, Doctors diets.
  Pothecaries Drugs, Surgeons Glisters,
  Stabbing of armes for a common Mistris,
  Riband favours. Ribauld Speeches,
  Deere perfumde Jacketts, pennylesse breeches,   190
  Dutch Flapdragons, healths in Urine,
  Drabs that keepe a man to sure in:
  I do defie you all.
  Lend me each honest hand, for here I rise,
  A reclaymde man loathing the generall vice.   195
HOORD. So, so, all friends, the wedding dinner cooles,
  Who seeme most crafty prove oft times most fooles.

FINIS.

TEXTUAL NOTES

SIGLA

Q1 = Quarto, 1608.
L1 = Copy of Q1 in B.M. (c.34.d.42).
L2 = Copy of Q1 in B.M. (Ashley 1158).
V1 = Copy of Q1 in Victoria and Albert Museum (6554.26. Box 33.1).
V2 = Copy of Q1 in Victoria and Albert Museum (6554.26. Box 33.2).
O1 = Copy of Q1 in Bodleian Library (Malone 797).
O2 = Copy of Q1 in Bodleian Library (Malone Add. 812).
E = Copy of Q1 in Library of Eton College.
Q2 = Edition of 1616.
DILKE = *Old Plays: Being a Continuation of Dodsley's Collection*, vol. 5, [ed. C. W. Dilke]. London, 1816.
DYCE = *The Works of Thomas Middleton, now first collected, with some account of the author, and notes, by the Reverend Alexander Dyce* (5 vols.). London, 1840.

DRAMATIS PERSONAE

There is no list of Dramatis Personae in Q1.

I.I

31   *Tarantula*,] tarantula, DYCE; *Tarantula*. Q1.
38   Forgive] Forgiue Q2; For giue Q1.
39   chide] Q2; chid Q1.
44   Curtizan] Q2; Currizan Q1.
53   som-thing,] somthing, Q2; som-thing_∧ Q1.
55   helpe you,] help you, Q2; helpe you_∧ Q1.
59   and] Q2; aud Q1.

99   now] DILKE; no Q1.
101 that?] Q2; ~; Q1.
121 sir?] Q2; ~: Q1.

I. II

41   money:] L1, L2, V1, V2, O1, O2; ~_∧ E.
46   purpose,] E; ~? L1, L2, V1, V2, O1, O2.
51   *hostis*] L1, L2, V1, V2, O1, O2; Hostis E.

I. III

6   Balsum] E; Balsamum L1, L2, V1, V2, O1, O2. *The form* Balsum

(=Balsam) *was rather new at this date; the proof-reader was unfamiliar with it, and emended to the commoner* Balsamum.

24 Nephew, *Lucre*] L1, L2, V1, V2, O1, O2; Nephew‿ *Lucre* E.
42 thee—] DYCE; ~, Q1.
65 upon't,] DILKE; vpon't‿ Q1.

I. IV

31 too‿] E; too; L1, L2, V1, V2, O1, O2.
46 Galleasses,] galleasses, DYCE; Galleasses‿ Q1.
50 reverend-honorable]; reuerend—honorable Q1.
55 agen—] again—DYCE; agen; Q1.
60 Foole-aminy] E; Fooli-aminy L1, L2, O1, O2, V1, V2. *The word occurs again at* IV. V. 106, *and is there spelt* fooleaminy.

II. I

ACT II] *Incipit* ACT. 2. Q1.
7 pennorth,] E; penworth: L1, L2, V1, V2, O1, O2. *The word occurs again at* III. IV. 29, *where it is spelt* pennort. *The form* penworth *probably results from the proof-reader's attempt to emend to a more "literary" or more "etymological" form.*
11 one] DILKE; owne Q1.
12 Translation—] ~‿ Q1.
14 SERVANT.] Ser. DILKE; Ser. 2. Q1.
38 *Staffordsheere?*] Staffordshire? DYCE; *Staffordsheere:* Q1.
51 faith.] DILKE; ~‿ L1, V2, O2, ~, L2, V1, O1, E.
95 have] haue Q2; hane Q1.
104 thinke] L1, L2, E, V2, O1, O2; thike V1.

105 unnaturall] vnnaturall Q2; vnnatnrall Q1.
116 you] Q2; your Q1.
129 HOST.] Host. Q2; Hostis. Q1.
163 deceaves] deceiues Q2; dceaues V1, decaues L1, L2, V2, O1, O2, E.
188 humour,] ~‿ Q1.
189 cheife] L1, L2, V2, O1, O2, E; chife V1. *Ten words earlier in the same line,* V1 *reads* from; *in the corrected copies this has been changed to* frō, *to make room for the extra letter in the line.*
196 comfort] Q2; comfott Q1.
196 S.D. *Enter* . . . WITT-GOOD] *placed after line* 197 *in* Q1.
205 Uncles] Vncles Q2; Vucles Q1.
205-7 You might . . . offence] *Lineated as in* DYCE; *in* Q1 *is printed as prose, but beginning a new line at* "You might", *and with an upper-case* "I" *in* "If". *The semicolon after* "blame" *may be the compositor's misreading of a mark made by Middleton to indicate the end of a line of verse: cf. in* Q1 *the colons at the end of* III. II. 7 *and* III. II. 9.
223 make-Match] Q2; make—Match Q1.
293 your] Q2; yours Q1.
315 then,] DILKE; ~; Q1.
344 faire standing] Q2; ~ stranding Q1.

II. II

34 surfetter] Q2; snrfetter Q1.
50 *Lucre*] Q2; *Lucer* Q1.
58 her?] Q2; ~. Q1.
59 Medler] L2, V1, V2, O1, O2, E; medler L1.

III. I

ACT III] *Incipit* ACT. 3. Q1.
82 then?] DILKE; ~. Q1.

IV. I] TEXTUAL NOTES

116 comfort] L2, V1, V2, O1, O2, E; comforr L1.
118 bestowd] bestow'd Q2; destowp L1, destowd L2, V1, V2, O1, O2, E.
120 first] L2, V1, V2, O1, O2, E; firist L1.
122 our] Q2; out Q1.
124 S.D. *Exeunt*] DYCE; *Exit* Q1.
124 S.D. GENTLEMEN] *Gentlemen* L2, V1, V2, O1, O2, E; *Gentleman* L1.
124 S.D. HOST ⟨*as*⟩ *servingman*] *Host as Servant* DYCE; *Host,— seruingman* Q1.
135 better] L2, V1, V2, O1, O2, E; bettre L1.
150 widdow—]; ~, Q1.
162 Gentlemen] L2, V1, V2, O1, O2, E; Centlemen L1.
166 overthrowen] ouerthrowne Q2; ouerthowen Q1.
171 beseech] Q2; besecch Q1.
173 HOORD.] *Hoard.* DILKE; *Ho.* (with catchword *Host*) Q1. *The printer's copy had the ambiguous* Ho., *which the compositor misinterpreted as* Host. *In* Q1, *Hoord's next speech-prefix (line* 190) *is also* Ho.,
217 sir—] DYCE; ~. Q1.
226 seeke,] seek, DYCE; seeke. Q1.
230 must] Q2; musi Q1.
233 Tedious-dissembling] Tedious—dissembling Q1.
233 very] Q2; very uery Q1.
242 suddenly] Q2; snddenly Q1.
249 engagde] engag'de Q2; engade Q1.
274 Merchants] merchant's DILKE; Mcrchants Q1.
275 possesse$_\wedge$] possess$_\wedge$ DILKE; possesse, Q1.
279 twelve$_\wedge$] twelue. Q1.
281 *Exeunt*] DILKE; *Exit* Q1.

III. II

7 enimy$_\wedge$] enemy$_\wedge$ DYCE; enimy: Q1. *See textual note on* II. I. 205–7.
9 so$_\wedge$] ~: Q1.
11 it] Q2; in Q1.

III. III

12 Mistres] Mistrcs Q1.
47 dinner?] Q2; ~$_\wedge$ Q1.
65 him—] ~. Q1.
66 Ile do] L2, E; I bee do L1, V1, V2, O1, O2. DILKE *cannot have seen a copy with this in the corrected state, and emended to* Ay boy, do, *followed by* DYCE.
75 the] DILKE; he Q1.
130 S.D. *Exit*] DYCE; *Eixt* Q1.

III. IV

12 bed] Q2; bed Bed Q1.
14 morning,] Q2; ~$_\wedge$ Q1.
16 Here] Q2; Hcre Q1.
23 prate] Q2; prat Q1. *There is a variant* prat, *but it is confined to Scotland.*
28 knew] Q2; knenw Q1.
31 this] Q2; ths Q1.
43 and] Q2; aud Q1.
46 cockscombrie] cockscombre Q1. *Cf. the forms* cockscombri (I. IV. 60) *and* cockscombry (III. IV. 54, IV. V. 103). *Middleton himself favoured* -ie *spellings; the compositor preferred* -y, *but sometimes reproduced the* -ie *of his copy: see Appendix. p.* 108.
64 *Audry?*] *Audrey?* DILKE; *Audry*$_\wedge$ Q1.

IV. I

ACT IV] *Incipit* ACT. 4. Q1.
1 In wedlocks bands] Q1 *leaves a space before this, suggesting that*

	it is intended as a separate line of verse, but I have left it unchanged, in conformity with lines 2 and 5 (*single long lines with internal rhyme*).
35	S.D. *Enter* LUCRE] *positioned as in* DILKE; Q1 *places it at line* 33.
53	friend] Q2 *emends to* friends; *but the* Q1 *form may be a survival of the uninflected plural (though admittedly this is not normal after the 14th Century).*
69	dry oake] Q2; dry, ~ Q1.

IV. II

41	wise,] DILKE; ~∧ Q1.
76	Ginnee] Girnne Q1. *The name also occurs at* II. I. 337, *where it is* Ginnee.

IV. III

40	cockscombs] cocskcombs Q1.
64	CREDITORS] *Cit.* Q1. *The* Q1 *form obviously means* Citizen(s); DILKE *and* DYCE *give the speech to the First Creditor, but it seems more likely that it is intended to be distributed among the three of them, in a babel of indignation.*
64	Puritanes,] ~∧ Q1.

IV. IV

4	hapines?] happiness? DILKE; hapines∧ Q1.
10	in troth] DILKE; introth Q1.
22	yet?] Q2; yer. Q1.
29	S.D. *Enter*] Q1 *has* "Enter All", *placed after line* 31.
54	your] Q2; you Q1.
64	perfumer—] ~: Q1.
76	Mistris] Q2; Mistrs Q1.
77	me?] DILKE; ~. Q1.
104	letter,] ~∧ Q1.

115	examine] Q2; ezamine Q1. *Muscular error or foul case: the boxes for* x *and for* z *were adjacent.*
133	drawne—within] ~ -within L1, L2, V2, O1, O2, E; ~, within V1.
135	SERVANT.] *Serv.* DILKE; I. Q1.
136	directions] Q2; derictions Q1.
169	roundly?] DILKE; ~. Q1.
190	Goose-giblet] Q2; Goose—giblet Q1.
206	Muligrubs] L1, L2, V2, O1, O2, E; Mulgraues V1. *The reading of the corrected copies,* Muligrubs, *is a thoroughly Middletonian name. The proof-reader must have referred to his copy, for there is nothing obviously wrong with* Mulgraues; *perhaps Middleton himself proof-read this page.*
242	Anthony] Q2; Anthory Q1.
253	immoveables] immoueables Q2; immouerables Q1.
274	all tast] ~ taste DILKE; ~ —tast Q1.
290	suspected, our] Q2; ~. our Q1.
291	*Exeunt*] DILKE; *placed on line* 290 *by* Q1.

IV. V

27	mullipoop] V1; mullipood L1, L2, V2, O1, O2, E. *The final letter of* mullipood *is an inverted* p; *the inversion probably took place accidentally when* concupiscenty *was corrected in the following line of* Q1.
28	concupiscency] L1, L2, V2, O1, O2, E; concupiscenty V1. *The compositor misread* c *as* t, *perhaps helped by the analogy of* concupiscent.
28	S.D. Gentlemen] Q2; Gentleman Q1.
73	Lancelot?] *Lancolot?* Q2; *Lancelot.* Q1.

TEXTUAL NOTES

100	spouting?] DILKE; ~. Q1.		11	Neece] Q2; Neecc Q1.
106	now?] DILKE; ~ₐ Q1.		28	*Hoord*, wife] Q2; ~. wife Q1.
108	sir—] DILKE; ~. —Q1.		33	Bride?] bride? DYCE; Bride. Q1.
111	sir—] Q2; ~. —Q1.		34	Maddam,] Madame, Q2; Maddamₐ Q1.
153	chaynes?] chaines? Q2; chaynesₐ Q1.		48	brother,] Q2; ~ₐ Q1.
170	shame—] Q2; ~.— Q1.		89	deepe,] deep, DILKE; deepeₐ Q1.
191	GULFE.] *Gul.* Q2; *Lul.* Q1.		101	Hoord—] Hoard— DYCE; Hoord: Q1.

v. I

A CT V] ACTVS. 5. Q1.

v. II

2	house?] DILKE; ~. Q1.
8	out?] DILKE; ~, Q1.
9	in order] Q2; inorder Q1.

119	abusde,] Q2; ~ₐ Q1.
125	me, I] Q2; ~ₐ I Q1.
137	forgiven] DILKE; for giuen Q1.
150	prickt in] Q2; prick tin Q1.
157	all,] Q2; ~. Q1.
162	of Toes] Q2; os Toes Q1.
174	tarry,] L1, L2, O1, E; ~ₐ V1, V2, O2.
190	breeches] Q2; breechcs Q1.

COMMENTARY

When quotations are given from Shakespeare, the line-references are from Peter Alexander's one-volume edition (London 1951)

I. I

This scene and the next are set in a town in the provinces.

7 Long-acre] The broad acres of Witt-good's lost estate.

7f. 3. yeares voyage] Playing on the idea of the capaciousness of his uncle's conscience: anyone who trusts himself to it is like a sailor embarking on a perilous voyage round the world. Cf. III. I. 191–5.

11 oxe-browde] Horned, and therefore cuckolds: a man whose wife had been unfaithful was said to wear horns. Cf. IV. IV. 83–4. 284.

23 sojourne upon their braine] Live by their wits.

75 set so good a courage on my state] "Make so good a showing" (Sampson).

86 a purpose] "on purpose". The play contains several examples of *a* used as the weak form of *on* and *of*, e.g. *a life* (II. I. 245, etc.), *peece a plate* (II. I. 343), *a this side* (III. I. 139), *ath Country* (IV. IV. 53), *a tother side* (IV. IV. 94–5), *A my troth* (IV. IV. 176, etc.), *alate* (IV. IV. 186), *set fire ath house* (IV. V. 124), *free ath Fishmongers* (V. II. 21–2), *hard a beleefe* (V. II. 105).

88–9 letts God alone with him] Refuses to help him, leaves him to the mercy of God.

91 Tis right the world] "That's exactly what the world is like."

92 kindnesse] Love, *i.e.* sexual performance.

98 turne all the waxe to hunny] Perhaps a reference to the story of Odysseus putting wax in the ears of his men so that they should not hear the song of the Sirens (*Odyssey* XII, 165ff.): Witt-good's story will dissolve the wax in the Host's ear so that he listens to him.

99 S.D. *Enter three* GENTLEMEN] This entrance is unmarked in Q1, and the speech-prefixes are simply 1., 2., and 3.. From the dialogue, it is clear that 1. is Onesiphorus Hoord; 2. and 3. are probably Kixe and Limber, who in V. II ride up to London with O.H. for his brother's wedding (cf. I. I. 134–9).

105 scarce see your selves] Presumably because of senility.

124 his wives Sonne and my Neece] *i.e.* Sam Freedome and Hoord's niece Joyce (who eventually marries Witt-good).

127 fall in] A pun: (*a*) make up a quarrel; (*b*) have sexual intercourse. The second meaning is not recorded in the *N.E.D.*, but its existence is clear from the same pun in Shakespeare's *Troilus and Cressida*: ". . . they two are twaine. —Falling in after falling out, may make them three [*i.e.* produce a child]" (III. I. 95–7).

136 violl betweene her legges] The viols were a family of six-stringed instruments somewhat resembling the modern violin family. The refer-

D

ence here is to the member of the family called the Viola da Gamba, which was held between the legs (like the modern cello).

139 A match, if it be a match?] "Agreed, if the wedding takes place."

I. II

4 Bully-Hadland] *Bully* was a term of familiar and convivial endearment among men. *Hadland* obviously means "one who did have land but no longer has".

9 spite of thy teeth] "Despite your opposition or resistance".

11 *Contra voluntatem et professionem*] "Against (your) inclination and profession".

15 Ginger] Was considered to be an aphrodisiac.

18 Pigs to a Parson] "As tithes" (Sampson).

30 a toung with a great T] With a capital T, *i.e.* "emphatically a tongue". Almost certainly there is also a phallic joke (everybody knew what widows liked best), but I have not been able to find an exact parallel.

51 H*ic et hæc hostis*] Punning on English *host* and Latin *hostis* "enemy": "If I don't stand you in good stead, then let the Host turn out to be a Hostis (enemy) to dicing etc.". It is of course unthinkable that a Host should be an enemy to such things. The *Hic et haec* comes from the grammar-books: in William Lily's Latin grammar (the only one that could legally be used in grammar schools), the nouns are all declined with the demonstrative in front of them, as if it were the definite article: *hic magister, haec musa,* etc.

If (like *hostis*) the noun can be either masculine or feminine, it is preceded (in the nominative) by *hic et haec*: so for example under the third declension we find *hic et haec parens.*

56 let off] Perhaps means "fire(d)", although this meaning is not recorded by the *N.E.D.* until 1714.

56 keepe full time] Musical metaphor: "(we) keep perfectly in time (with each other)".

I. III

The scene has now moved to London, where it remains for the rest of the play.

12 as a Bawd] Like a pander, *i.e.* standing by without participating.

13 wipes his nose of] Cheats him of.

19 in the evening of] Towards the end of.

28 *Vulnera delacerata*] Literally "wounds torn in pieces", *i.e.* "lacerating wounds". I have been unable to trace the source, which is probably post-classical. Hoord's translation *delacerate* is his own coinage: it presumably means "lacerating".

32 lye by't] Perhaps "lie sick because of it", or possibly "take the consequences of it".

56 take of] *i.e.* "take off".

73 Chancery] The Court of Chancery, which could give remedy where none existed in common law, or where common-law remedy was denied (*e.g.* by intimidation). The *boxe* is of course the blow that Monylove had given him.

I. IV

4 S.D. DAMPIT and GULFE] Dampit's name is compounded

from *damn* and *pit*; the latter word could mean "dungeon", "grave", "pitfall, trap", and (in *the pit*) "Hell". The word *gulfe* was often applied to a voracious appetite, and to the bellies of predatory animals.

22 stakte his Mastie] Presumably Dampit had arranged a dog-fight, and had staked the dog itself as his wager.

32 oh maister *Dampit*] Probably a parenthetical greeting called out to Dampit, the phrases before and after being addressed at Dampit but not heard by him.

35 the Poets tell us] *e.g.* Seneca, in whose plays this is one of the recurrent moral maxims.

45 *Westminster* hall] Here sat the three common law courts—king's bench, common pleas, and exchequer.

57–8 Motions of Fleete-streete, and Visions of Holborne] A *motion* was a puppet-show, or a puppet. Sampson thinks that the puppets and the visions are both contemptuous references to Dampit's clients, and he glosses *Visions* as "mere images". *Vision* however is not usually a pejorative word. Perhaps there is some reference to the London law-university: of the fourteen Inns, no less than nine were in Fleet Street or Holborn. But Dampit's flamboyant language, as often, is obscure to the modern reader.

65 souc'st] *i.e.* soused, drenched. Perhaps also "imposed upon, swindled", though the *N.E.D.* does not record this meaning before the 18th century.

II. I

8 halfe in halfe] "Half the total amount." He is calculating the extent to which he had swindled Witt-good.

11–12 the last Translation] The latest metaphor, or change of meaning. *Translatio* ("metaphor") was a technical term of rhetoric.

19 calles me theefe] *Good fellow* was a cant term for "thief".

31 first flight] Commonly used of fledglings leaving the nest: this is the first time the widow has left her estate and come up to London.

32 Tearme businesse] Legal business of the kind to be transacted during term, *i.e.* while the law-courts were sitting; but with overtones from the fact that prostitutes also congregated in London in term-time.

35 Medler] Suggesting both "meddler" and "medlar". The medlar was a small stone-fruit, eaten when rotten, and was also slang for the female pudenda. Cf. *Romeo and Juliet* II. 1. 33–6.

52 take me with you] "Let me understand you; explain to me."

62–3 goe downe] A pun: (*a*) leave London; (*b*) go to bed with a lover.

66 give her that gift] "Grant her that" (Sampson).

98 unknowe] "Unknown". The tone is one of incredulous astonishment: "Fancy suggesting that he is unknown!".

118 have my coate pull'd ore my eares] Perhaps, as Sampson says, so that he could be whipped; but it could mean "have my coat removed", *i.e.* "be dismissed from service".

144–5 cloake companions ... blew coates] Lucre first uses *companions* in its pejorative sense ("scurvy fellows"), and then adds that *companions* ("associates") is the right word for such servants, because they dress as if they were the equals of their masters. He is deploring the tendency for servants to wear cloaks instead of the traditional livery-coats.

163 he deceaves me) "I am mistaken about him".

181 put worship upon him] Treat him respectfully, call him "your worship".

205 knowne] Been acquainted with, *i.e.* used, visited.

213 take it in that sence] Interpret it like that.

235–6 feare neither Beadle nor Somner] *i.e.* go in no fear of punishment for sexual licence. The duties of the beadle included the whipping of whores (see *King Lear*, IV. VI. 160–1). The somner (summoner) was an official who haled offenders before the ecclesiastical courts.

236 coale-harbour] The Coldharbour, originally a large house on the north bank of the Thames, two or three hundred yards west of London Bridge. In the late 16th century it had been pulled down by the Earl of Shrewsbury, its then owner, who "in place thereof builded a great number of smal tenements now letten out for great rents, to people of all sortes" (John Stow, *A Survey of London*, ed. C. L. Kingsford, Vol. I, p. 237. Oxford (Clarendon Press) 1908). It was notorious as a sanctuary, and as a place where hasty marriages could be solemnised.

248–9 take me handsomely] "Interprets me courteously", or perhaps "pleases me well".

297–8 by my fathers occupation] By *fathers* he means "step-father's"; Sam's status has risen since his mother's remarriage to Lucre, who is a gentleman by birth.

299 by my Fathers Coppy) A copyholder held land by custom of the manor, and had a copy of the court rolls on which his rights were recorded. His son had the right to succeed to the holding on his father's death (on payment of the prescribed fine) and so could be said to hold "by his father's copy". Here of course figurative.

299 the Charter] The reference to "the 15 page" suggests that he is talking about a printed charter; this rules out the Charter of the City of London, which did not get printed until later in the 17th century; perhaps Sam is referring to Magna Carta, which was frequently reprinted. Needless to say, there is nothing in it corresponding to his comic gloss.

339 good Rubbish] *i.e.* land.

359–60 the right worshipfull; all the twelve companyes] The twelve principal Livery Companies of London (Mercers, Grocers, Drapers, Fishmongers, Goldsmiths, Skinners, Merchant Taylors, Haberdashers, Salters, Ironmongers Vintners, and Clothworkers).

372 make a Bolt, or a shaft ont] Take a risk and accept the outcome, "have a go" (proverbial).

II. II

6 stood otherwise affected] "Was otherwise inclined", or "loved somebody else".

19–20 for your words will passe] This is parenthetical, and in modern punctuation would be put in brackets or between dashes. *Passe* could mean "find a passage" or "succeed" or "excel".

20 set faire for] Stand a good chance of.
49 plauge] *i.e.* "plague". Q2 corrects to *plague*, but *plauge* is in fact Middleton's own spelling, as can be seen from the Trinity MS of *A Game at Chess*.

III. I

23 be content] *i.e.* to "remove" him (line 17).
28 Would twere ... with] "I wish you owed us as much as we would dare to lend you without security."
55 play the maide] *i.e.* yield after a seemly display of resistance. Cf. Shakespeare, *Richard III*: "Play the Maids part, still answer nay, and take it" (III. VII. 51).
91 Muscadine and eggs] "The mixture of muscadine and eggs was taken as an aphrodisiac" (Bullen).
99 have the better tearme] *i.e.* like a lawyer having a profitable term: punning on the two meanings of *suitor* (legal and amorous). See also note on II. I. 32.
120 I reach at farder happines] *i.e.* at marriage with the Neece, so that the Curtizan is "free" to go off and marry Hoord.
133 saving my selfe harmelesse] "Provided it doesn't get me into trouble."
134 thou shalt heare better from me] *i.e.* I shall reward you better.
155 their desarts] *i.e.* Witt-good's and Lucre's.
164 in appearing forme] In outward appearance.
175 neither of us] This shows that there are only *two* gentlemen with Hoord, whereas later *three* gentlemen argue about their parts in this persuasion: see note on III. III. 33.

182 his due body] An unusual use of *due*; presumably means "which his creditors are legally entitled to seize on".
204 at the bound] This usually meant "at the first opportunity", but here seems to mean rather "on the rebound".
220 a chin not worth a haire] *i.e.* a beardless boy.
221 clap hands] It was customary for two people to strike hands reciprocally as a token that they agreed on a bargain.
223 your labour, and thy love] *Your* to the gentlemen, *thy* (singular) to the Curtizan.

III. II

14 a private charge] "An order to deliver secretly" (Sampson).

III. III

2 Pomgranite] It was customary for the rooms of inns to be given such names; cf. Shakespeare's *Henry IV*. I: "looke downe into the Pomgarnet, *Ralfe*" (II. IV. 35–6).
23 tooke her at best vantage] Attacked her from the most favourable position (military metaphor).
33 THIRD GENTLEMAN.] The S.D. at the beginning of the scene marks the entry of *two* gentlemen, and there were only two gentlemen with Hoord in III. I. (see note on III. I. 175). As this is the only speech attributed to the third gentleman, it might be thought that *3.* was a compositor's error for *2.*, were it not that Hoord replies "you did *all* well" (contrasted with his earlier "you did *both* well"). It seems probable therefore that the inconsistency

existed in Middleton's manuscript, so I have let it stand in the text.
51–2 has his part with-out booke] Has learnt it by heart.
68 give two for one] Give better than they get.
93 to Boate] This is a slip by Wittgood, since he ought not to know that she had taken boat; he says it to make sure that the Host will be able to track down the fugitives.

III. IV

2 Anno. 99.] Dyce emends to 89, and Sampson to 98, because violent storms are recorded in those years.
4 Poovyes new buildings] This is more likely to refer to something topical (1605–6) than to something in 1599. In 1605, James I ordered that no more houses in the City should be built of wood, and Sampson has found a reference (unfortunately not exactly dated) to a leather-seller who put up a timber building in Paul's Churchyard, and was obliged to pull it down. Sampson has also shown that in the reign of James I there was a leather-seller in the City named Povey. It is therefore possible that it was Povey who was concerned in the Paul's Churchyard affair, which at the time may well have been a *cause célèbre*.
22 mought, and you would] "Could if you wished."
28 I nere knew you do otherwise] By *naught* ("badly") Dampit had meant "in bad health", but Audry (perversely) takes it to mean "wickedly".
47 Cavernesed] One of Dampit's bombastic nonce-words. It is perhaps compounded from *cavern* and *eased* (as *e.g.* of the bowels). In Q1,

admittedly, it comes at a line-division, and is divided *Cavernesed*; but this is not conclusive, since the compositor himself may well have been baffled by it.
50 doubts nothing but] "Fears nothing except".
57–8 Misters Proserpine] Presumably Dampit's landlady, to whom Audry is servant. Middleton's usual spelling is *Mistris*, but cf. the rhyme *Glisters* / *Mistris* (v. ii. 187–8).
61 the liberties] The area subject to the control of the London civic authorities.
67 Barnards Inne] One of the Inns of Chancery, in Holborn.

IV. I

28 Upon calme conditions] "On condition that he undertakes to behave calmly."
58 furnisht of his needes] "Provided with bare necessities."
69 dry oake] *i.e.* Hoord.
79 FIRST GENTLEMAN.] This is not the same First Gentleman as in lines 1–5, but *Lucre's* first gentleman. Another example of Middleton's carelessness with the minor characters.

IV. II

5–6 gallant Dicer ... pennance] The dicer has gambled away his doublet, and so looks like a penitent performing an act of mortification. In Middleton's *Your Five Gallants*, there is in fact a scene (II. III) where a gallant is stripped down to his shirt at dice.
9 Hyegate] Highgate, now inside London, but then a village well outside, and so the kind of place

[IV. IV]   COMMENTARY   95

where a wealthy citizen might well have a country house.

65–6 Pray let ... trust] If the estate were given to Witt-good in trust, ownership of it would not have been transferred to him; he is very quick to pick up this point, and obtain acknowledgment from Lucre that ownership *has* been transferred. Perhaps (since the Host is still present) the lines are spoken aloud, to force his uncle's hand.

90 envie] With second-syllable stress, normal for *envy* as a verb at this date.

IV. III

9 thrumb-chind] A jocular word for "bearded". A *thrum* is the fringe of threads at the edge of a piece of cloth.

19 cast your cap at] "Give up all hopes of".

22–3 a hole ith counter] The two Counters were the sheriff's prisons in London, to which debtors were consigned. The *hole* was the ward for the poorest prisoners (see Stow, *Survey of London*, ed. Kingsford, I. 115).

38 loose all that] *i.e.* lose all the money etc. that they had given him in III. I.

40 *Non plus ultra*] "The extreme limit". A conflation of two common phrases, *Ne plus ultra* and *Non ultra*.

41 were] *i.e.* "we're".

46 beasts know no reasonable time] "Animals experience no time when they are rational"—because by definition man alone is *animal rationale*.

62 in hell] Debtors' prisons were called "hell".

64 Puritanes] At this date used only as a term of opprobrium, by opponents of puritanism.

IV. IV

13 chashocks] Otherwise unrecorded, but presumably a variant of *cassock*, "a cloak or long coat worn by a horseman". *Chashock* may be a vulgarism; for dialectal or vulgar *sh* for *s*, see E. J. Dobson, *English Pronunciation* 1500–1700, vol. II, p. 947. Oxford (Clarendon Press) 1957.

43 Sa ho] A cry used in coursing, but here used as a falconer's cry.

45 There boy] Huntsman's cry to his dogs. Cf. Shakespeare's *Tempest*, IV. I. 256.

90 præcontract] An agreement to marry, forming a canonical impediment to subsequent marriage to another person. A precontract could be set aside only with the agreement of both parties.

139 deeper then the desperate state] She has reached the state of despair and then gone beyond it. Cf. I. I. 63–4.

163–4 far stronger then the first] *The first* cannot mean her marriage-vow to Hoord, since the whole point is that that was not first; presumably Witt-good pretends that he is going to remind her of a promise of marriage (to himself) even stronger than the one mentioned in the letter.

169 come of] *i.e.* come off ("pay up").

189–90 set the Hares head to the Goose-giblet] Balance off one thing against another (proverbial).

206 Muligrubs] The name means "fit of melancholy or spleen".

226 eight score od pounds] Does not tally with IV. III. 28–31, according to which he owes them £190.

250 Dove-holes] "Dovehouses". The word is still quite common in dialect, especially in northern England.

260 our destiny] Hanging and wiving were said to go by destiny, and this gives ironic point to Hoord's cheerful concurrence.

283 short-pig-hayrde] Citizens wore their hair short.

IV. V

2 *pits enow to dam him*] Referring to the name *Dampit* (see note to I. IV. 4). The primary meaning of *pits* here can hardly be "dungeons": there were no prisons in Fleet Street or Holborn. It perhaps means "pitfalls, traps", with a specific reference to lawyers (see note to I. IV. 57–8).

5 *Trahe, traheto*] Imperative of Latin *trahere*: either singular and plural (*trahe, trahite*), or the two forms of the imperative singular (*trahe, trahito*). *Trahere* means "draw" (including "draw a drink").

6 S.D. *Enter Gentlemen*] In what follows, there are numerous passages of dialogue which are not heard by Dampit; the context shows clearly enough which these are, and I have not felt it necessary to mark them as asides.

7–8 like the devill in chaines] See *Revelation* XX. 2. Dampit, now quite incapacitated by drinking, is held up in bed by some kind of adjustable contraption of chains and rods (cf. "set me up a pegge higher", lines 103–4).

27 gernative] Nonce-word formed from the verb *to girn* ("to snarl, grumble, grin"); so "snarling", "grumbling", or "grinning".

27 mullipoop] One of Dampit's nonce-words, formed on the pattern of *mullipuff* "fuzzball" (also used of persons). *Mully* meant "dusty, powdery". *Poop* could mean "posteriors, rump"; this is not recorded in the *N.E.D.* before 1645, but is the kind of vulgar word that would be in oral use without getting into print. There was also a verb *to poop*, which meant "to deceive, cheat". The *N.E.D.*'s *mullipood* is a ghost-word.

31–2 the Taverne bitch . . . head] *i.e.* "he is drunk" (proverbial).

51 unfetherd cremitoryed] One of the traditional descriptions of man was "an unfeathered biped"; here perhaps suggesting "unfledged". *Cremitoryed*, another nonce-word, is quite opaque.

74 Pythagoricall] Reference to Pythagoras's theory of transmigration of souls: as a soul takes a different body, so Sir Lancelot changes his outer garment (to avoid being recognised and arrested for debt).

86 farewell and a thousand] A thousand farewells.

91 upon departing] Just about to fail.

104 a pegge higher] See note to lines 7–8 above.

110 device] Deliberate malapropism for *advice*.

119 *ejectione firme*] A writ giving repossession of landed property. "*Qvare eiecit infra terminum*, is a writ, and it lyeth where one maketh a lease to another for term of yeeres, and the lessor infeoffeth an other, and the feoffee putteth out the termor, then the termor shall haue this writ against the feoffee. But if an other stranger put

out the termor, then he shall haue a writ *de Eiectione firme* against him. And in these two writs he shall recouer the terme & his damages" (John Rastell, *An Exposition of . . . Termes of the Lawes*. London, 1607).
123 this geere will fadge well] "This business will turn out well" (ironical).
125 breake strife] "End contention".
147 keepes open house] Dampit's phrase carries a sexual innuendo, which is unnoticed by Hoord as he innocently enlarges on it.
154–5 *monstrum . . . ademptum*] "A monster, terrible, hideous, gigantic, from whom the light (had been) withdrawn" (of the giant Polyphemus after his blinding, *Aeneid* III. 658).
163 the welch Embassador] The cuckoo was commonly called "the Welsh ambassador", originally perhaps because, in Welsh literary tradition, it was a messenger of love. See Gwyn Williams, "The Cuckoo, the Welsh Ambassador", in *M.L.R.*, LI (1956), pp. 223–5.
165 in my naked bed] "When I am naked in bed". It was common to sleep naked.
170 Ant twere] *Ant* is *And* ("if") with *d* assimilated to *t* by the following voiceless consonant.

v. ii

8 cupbard of plate] Service of plate, set of vessels displayed on a sideboard.
21–2 free ath Fishmongers] *i.e.* admitted to the privileges of the Fishmongers' Company. The names *Spichcocke* ("broiled eel") and *Lamprey* are indicative of their fishmongering ancestry.

42–3 an other antient Gentleman] In fact *two* gentlemen come in with O. Hoord; another example of carelessness of detail.
43 S.D. KIXE] The name means "a dry stalk", and so "a dried-up, sapless person".
58 stuck sore] "Persisted strongly", or possibly "wounded severely".
82 By your leave] A polite way of saying farewell.
108 *Negatur Argumentum*] "(Your) argument is denied". Latin was still used for disputation at the universities.
109 *Probo tibi*] "I prove (it) to you".
111 *ergo*] "Therefore".
112 *Negatur, sequela majoris*] "The implication of (your) major (premise) is denied".
119 Junt] Otherwise unrecorded. The *N.E.D.* glosses "trick", deriving it from Italian *giunta* "a cheat"; this fits well with the play's insistence on the word *trick* (*e.g.* IV. IV. 213, 281).
128 forc'st] "Forced". A typical Middleton spelling (see Appendix).
136 Thanke] The change from verse to prose comes on a new page (H3v), which is suspicious; moreover, the catchword on H3 is *Thanke*, whereas H3v begins with *thanke*. However, if the rest of the speech was originally in verse, the lineation is by no means obvious, and I retain the prose of Q1.
167 Fayning excuse to weomens Labours] "Pretending that we are going to assist at a child-birth."
170 tho signe be at heart] *i.e.* not hesitating to be let blood even though the time is astrologically unpropitious for it. Each sign of the Zodiac corresponded to a part of the human body, Leo corresponding to the heart and back.

"Item no part of a mans body ought to be touched with any Chirurgical instrument or Cauteri, actual, or potential, when the Sonne, or Moone, or the lorde of the Ascendent, is in the same signe that ruleth that part of mans body" (John Securis, *An Almanacke*. Salisbury, 1574).

186 Queanes Evills] *i.e.* venereal diseases. There is doubtless also a play on *King's Evil* ("scrofula"). Admittedly, *queen* and *quean* still had different vowels in educated southern speech (see Dobson, *English Pronunciation* II, p. 640); but Witt-good may well be playing on a dialectal/vulgar pronunciation of *quean*.

188 Stabbing of armes] It was a practice for gallants to draw their own blood and drink it as a health to their mistresses.

191 Dutch Flapdragons] Flapdragons were small objects (*e.g.* raisins) taken from burning spirit and swallowed flaming. The Dutch were said to be particularly expert.

192 keepe a man to sure in] Probably "imprison a man too securely".

BIBLIOGRAPHY

ABBREVIATIONS

J.E.G.P. = *Journal of English and Germanic Philology*
M.L.N. = *Modern Language Notes*
M.L.Q. = *Modern Language Quarterly*
M.L.R. = *Modern Language Review*
N. & Q. = *Notes and Queries*
P.M.L.A. = *Publications of the Modern Languages Association of America*
R.E.S. = *Review of English Studies*

I. Works by Middleton
A. GENERAL

The Works of Thomas Middleton, ed. Alexander Dyce (5 vols.). London, 1840.

The Works of Thomas Middleton, ed. A. H. Bullen (8 vols.). London, 1885–86.

Thomas Middleton, ed. Havelock Ellis, in the Mermaid Series (2 vols.). London, 1887–90. This edition contains ten plays.

Thomas Middleton, ed. Martin W. Sampson. New York (American Book Co.) 1915. Contains *Michaelmas Term*, *A Trick to Catch the Old One*, *A Fair Quarrel*, and *The Changeling*.

B. *A TRICK TO CATCH THE OLD ONE*

A Trick to Catch the Old One: Quarto, 1608; Octavo(?), 1616.

Old Plays; Being a Continuation of Dodsley's Collection, vol. 5, [ed. C. W. Dilke]. London, 1816.

II. Studies by Others
A. GENERAL
1. Critical

BALD, R. C. "The Sources of Middleton's City Comedies", in *J.E.G.P.*, xxxiii (1934), pp. 373–87.

——. "The Chronology of Middleton's Plays", in *M.L.R.*, xxxii (1937), pp. 33–43.

BARKER, R. H. *Thomas Middleton*. New York and London (Columbia U.P., Oxford U.P.) 1958.

BRADBROOK, M. C. *Themes and Conventions of Elizabethan Tragedy*. Cambridge (Cambridge U.P.) 1935.

——. *The Growth and Structure of Elizabethan Comedy*. London (Chatto and Windus) 1955.

BULLOCK, H. B. "Thomas Middleton and the Fashion in Playmaking", in *P.M.L.A.*, XLII (1927), pp. 766–76.

CHRISTIAN, M. G. "Middleton's acquaintance with the *Merrie Conceited Jests of George Peele*", in *P.M.L.A.*, L (1935), pp. 753–60.

ELLIS-FERMOR, U.M. *The Jacobean Drama*. Revised edition, London (Methuen) 1958.

ELIOT, T. S. "Thomas Middleton", in *Selected Essays*, London (Faber) 1932.

FISHER, M. "Notes on the Sources of some Incidents in Middleton's London Plays", in *R.E.S.*, XV (1939), pp. 283–93.

KNIGHTS, L. C. *Drama and Society in the Age of Jonson*. London (Chatto and Windus) 1937.

LYNCH, K. *The Social Mode of Restoration Comedy*, in University of Michigan Publications, *Language and Literature*, vol. III. New York and London (Michigan U.P.) 1926.

PARKER, R. B. "Middleton's Experiments with Comedy and Judgement", in *Stratford-upon-Avon Studies* I (1960), *Jacobean Theatre*, ed. J. R. Brown and B. Harris.

POWER, W. "Thomas Middleton vs. King James I", in *N. & Q.*, IV (1957), pp. 526–34.

——. "Middleton's Way with Names", in *N. & Q.*, VII (1960), pp. 26–9, 56–60, 95–8, 136–40, 175–9.

SCHOENBAUM, S. *Middleton's Tragedies*, New York (Columbia U.P.) 1955.

——. "*A Chaste Maid in Cheapside* and Middleton's City Comedy", in *Studies in English Renaissance Drama*, ed. J. W. Bennett *et al.* London (Peter Owen and Vision Press) 1959.

SCOTT-KILVERT, I. "Thomas Middleton", in *Nine*, II (1950), pp. 315–27.

SYMONS, A. "Middleton and Rowley", in *The Cambridge History of English Literature*, vol. VI, ed. A. W. Ward and A. R. Waller. Cambridge (Cambridge U.P.) 1910.

B. *A TRICK TO CATCH THE OLD ONE*

1. Critical

CRUIKSHANK, A. H. *Philip Massinger*, pp. 205–8. Oxford (Clarendon Press) 1920. He compares *A Trick to Catch the Old One* with *A New Way to Pay Old Debts*.

LEVIN, R. "The Dampit Scenes in *A Trick to Catch the Old One*", in *M.L.Q.*, XXV (1964), pp. 140–52.

2. Bibliographical

PRICE, G. R. "The Early Editions of *A Trick to catch the old one*", in *The Library*, 5th series, XXII (1967), pp. 205–27.

GLOSSARY

a	*on, of (see note to* I. I. 86).
affect	*love,* III. II. 8, IV. I. 52.
affection	*bias, partiality* III. I. 169.
afront	*confront, defy,* I. III. 3.
againe, against	*by the time that,* II. I. 341, III. III. 53.
an, and	*if,* II. I. 189, 270, 272, III. IV. 22, IV. III. 55, IV. V. 67.
angell	*gold coin worth ten shillings,* II. I. 125.
anon	*immediately* (="*coming, at your service*"), II. I. 148, III. III. 46, 61.
ant	*if,* IV. V. 170; *if it,* II. I. 118 etc.
approve	*prove,* III. I. 112.
arras	*cloth of arras: tapestry hangings round walls of a room,* II. I. 324.
aspick	*asp, poisonous snake,* I. III. 51.
ath	*of the, on the (see note to* I. I. 86).
aunt	*bawd, procuress,* II. I. 10, 11.
babliaminy	*babbler (nonce-word),* IV. V. 51.
back-racket	*the return of a ball in tennis,* IV. IV. 197.
balsum	*balsam, balm,* I. III. 6.
bargayne	*beating the bargayne: haggling* I. I. 118.
baudreaminy	*bawdry (nonce-word),* III. IV. 47.
beare downe	*overrule, insist,* III. III. 25.
bed-red	*bed-rid,* IV. V. 13 etc.
bedstaff(e)	*stout stick used to support bedding on a bedstead,* IV. V. 9, 153.
beholding	*beholden, under obligation,* II. I. 265, 314, III. I. 73, 248.
berlady	*by our lady,* IV. II. 45.
blew(-)coate	*livery,* II. I. 145; *liveried servingman,* III. I. 127.
bloud	*passion, sexual desire,* III. I. 72.
border	*piece of ornamental work on a garment,* IV. IV. 252.
bosome	*intimate, beloved,* IV. V. 66.
bottes	*horse-maggots,* I. I. 66.
breath	*breathing-space,* IV. III. 32.
brothell	*harlot,* I. I. 6, III. I. 90; *worthless, degenerate,* I. IV. 13.
brothell-maister	*whoremaster,* I. III. 26-7, II. I. 194.
bulbeggar	*hobgoblin, bogy,* I. IV. 69.
busse	*kiss,* IV. V. 63.
cald in	*collected,* IV. IV. 229.
canary	*a light sweet wine from the Canaries,* IV. V. 138.

carry	take, conduct, II. I. 326, III. III. 85, etc; carry it away: *win the day*, III. I. 82.
censure	opinion, judgment, III. I. 176.
champion-grounds:	open country, unenclosed land, IV. IV. 51.
circumstance	(detailed) story, I. I. 97.
clap	clap it up: *conclude the bargain hastily*, II. I. 259, III. I. 243.
cleanely	cleverly, neatly, I. I. 70, IV. IV. 111.
cleere	free, unmarried, IV. I. 91.
clos(s)e	secret, II. I. 256 etc.; secretly, V. II. 166.
closse stoole	commode, chamber-pot, IV. V. 176-7.
coades-nigs	God's nigs (meaningless oath), II. I. 305.
coale-harbour	see note on II. I. 236
cocks-combri(e)	foolery, folly, III. IV. 46 etc.; fools (collectively), I. IV. 60.
cod-peice	bag-shaped appendage at the front of a man's breeches, I. IV. 55.
compasse	reach, I. I. 28
conceave	(a) understand, (b) become pregnant, I. I. 58.
conceite	ingenious (odd?) method, IV. V. 11.
conceive	understand, IV. II. 49.
confound	destroy, ruin, II. I. 44, III. I. 13.
confusion	ruin, destruction, IV. IV. 159.
conjurer	practiser of black magic, I. II. 13.
consort	(a) band of musicians, (b) husband, I. I. 137.
consume	perish, III. I. 17.
coosenage	(a) cheating, (b) kinship, IV. II. 98.
co(o)zen, couzen	cheat, defraud, I. I. 80 etc.
coulour	gloss over, excuse, II. I. 214.
countenance	standing, dignity, II. I. 225; favour, patronage, IV. IV. 48; patron, supporter, II. II. 19.
country	district, neighbourhood, I. I. 100.
cranck	aggressive, cocky, I. III. 69.
crosse	thwart, oppose, I. III. 42 etc.
cuds me	God's me (meaningless oath), II. I. 39 etc.
cullisance	badge, emblem, IV. V. 52.
cunny-borrowe	rabbit-burrow, IV. IV. 251.
cunnycatching	cheating, III. IV. 37.
dasht	splashed, bespattered, I. IV. 44.
dauber	plasterer, II. I. 301.
day	delay, III. I. 267; longer day: *longer time to repay a debt*, IV. V. 81; the longest day of one's life: *as long as one lives*, I. III. 71, III. III. 20.
defeate	ruin, defraud, I. III. 24.
defie	renounce, V. II. 159, 193.
demise	conveyance of property, IV. IV. 248.
devized	thought of, III. I. 237.
dispatchfull	quickly killing, II. II. 49.

GLOSSARY

drab	*harlot*, I. I. 52 etc.; *to whore*, I. III. 32.
drawer	*tapster*, III. III. 1 etc.
du(t)ch widdow	*prostitute*, III. III. 15 etc.
embrion	*embryo*, I. I. 53.
entertaine	*take into one's service*, IV. IV. 15 etc.
estate	*endow, make a settlement on*, II. II. 73 etc.
even-minded	*impartial*, I. III. 10.
examiner	*official of Court of Chancery who took depositions of witnesses*, I. IV. 52.
executions	*writs of execution, arrest-warrants*, III. I. 181.
expresse	*show, manifest*, IV. II. 78.
fadomes	*depths*, III. I. 195.
fancy	*love*, V. II. 162.
fasten upon	*persuade to accept*, II. I. 357.
fetch over	*get the better of*, I. I. 116.
fit	*supply, furnish*, II. I. 74.
follow	*follow up, prosecute*, V. II. 129.
foole-aminy	*fool*, IV. V. 106; *fools (collectively)*, I. IV. 60.
fread	*frightened*, V. II. 71.
froat	*rub with perfumes*, IV. III. 28.
galleasse	*heavy low-built warship*, I. IV. 46.
game	*(a) gambling, (b) amorous adventures*, V. II. 182.
glister	*clyster*, V. II. 187.
guesse	*guests*, V. II. 52, 53.
gulle	*dupe, simpleton*, III. I. 139.
gullery	*trickery*, IV. I. 27.
hard	*nearby*, I. II. 54.
hit of	*hit on, remember the name of*, II. I. 97.
honesty	*chastity*, I. I. 37.
hower	*at an hower: punctual*, V. II. 46.
humour	*disposition*, II. I. 188.
I	*aye, yes*, I. I. 130 etc.
inconscionable	*unconscionable*, IV. V. 167.
indifferences	*impartiality*, I. III. 10.
infortunity	*adversity*, III. IV. 45.
insteed	*in (good) stead*, I. II. 51; *instead*, I. III. 6.
intelligencer	*spy*, II. I. 132.
interest in	*influence with*, II. I. 237.
lap	*tie up, entangle*, I. III. 24.
law-quillit	*legal quibble*, I. I. 10.
lay	*search*, I. II. 3.

leash	*a leash of: three*, II. I. 125.
lie	*lodge*, II. I. 126.
lighting	*lightning*, III. IV. 3.
living	*income, property, estate*, I. I. 22 etc.
longer, longest	*see* day.
lordship	*manor, estate*, III. I. 275, IV. I. 59.
lustie	*merry, handsome*, II. I. 84.
making	*betrothal*, III. III. 71.
marke	*monetary unit of thirteen shillings and fourpence*, III. I. 135, IV. IV. 232.
marquesse	*marchioness*, IV. IV. 83.
mastie	*mastiff*, I. IV. 15, 22.
matcht	*married*, III. I. 197.
meere	*complete, absolute, downright*, I. III. 10, II. I. 25, III. III. 116.
meerely	*entirely*, IV. II. 37.
misse	*lack*, IV. II. 94.
muckinder	*handkerchief*, IV. V. 12.
mull-sack	*mulled sack (q.v.)*, I. I. 68.
muscadine	*a strong sweet wine*, III. I. 91 etc.
neere	*never*, II. I. 36 etc.; *near*, II. I. 237.
nere	*never*, I. I. 8 etc.; *near* IV. V. 105.
nibled	*caught, cheated*, I. IV. 31.
noble	*gold coin worth six shillings and eightpence*, I. IV. 22.
nonsute	*reject the suit of*, II. I. 89.
nuncle	*uncle*, V. II. 156.
officious	*obliging, zealous*, I. I. 86.
once	*for once*, IV. IV. 199.
ordnary	*fixed-price meal at a public eating-house*, I. I. 5.
outlanders	*(a) foreigners, (b) things that put a man out of his land*, V. II. 183.
out-monies	*sums out on loan, or otherwise not in hand*, II. II. 50–1.
over-looke	*superintend*, V. II. 13.
owers	*rowing-boats*, I. IV. 47.
passion	*violent emotion (especially of sorrow)*, IV. II. 19.
paste	*pastry*, IV. II. 81.
pawne	*security for a loan*, III. I. 276.
pax	*pox*, II. I. 97 etc.
peevish	*foolish*, IV. IV. 189.
perforce	*by (physical) force*, I. III. 54.
phraze	*style, phraseology*, II. II. 37, 47.
pig-eater	*gentile (used as a term of endearment)*, IV. I. 7.
plot	*secret scheme*, II. I. 347 etc.; *scene-by-scene summary of the action of a play (used in the theatre)*, II. I. 349.

GLOSSARY

policy	*crafty trick*, II. II. 48; *craftiness*, IV. III. 39.
possesse	*put in possession of*, III. I. 275.
practise	*trickery, intrigue*, I. I. 12.
præmunire	*a writ ordering a sheriff to summon a person to answer a charge*, I. I. 10.
pregnant	*resourceful*, III. I. 123.
presently	*immediately*, II. I. 321.
president	*precedent*, IV. I. 49.
prethe(e)	*prithee, I pray you*, I. II. 35 etc.
priggin	*thieving, haggling*, III. III. 51.
promise	*assure*, III. I. 225; *assure you*, III. I. 256.
proper	*handsome, elegant*, II. I. 65, 165, III. I. 126.
punke	*prostitute*, I. II. 17.
purchase	*booty, spoil*, I. I. 116 etc.
push	*pshaw*, II. I. 102 etc.
qualities	*accomplishments, skills*, IV. IV. 16.
queane	*impudent woman, hussy*, III. IV. 47 etc.; *whore*, V. I. 17 etc.
rackt	*with their rents increased extortionately*, I. I. 34.
ram-headed	*(a) thick-witted, (b) cuckolded*, IV. IV. 284.
remember	*remind*, III. I. 230 etc.
reputted	*reputed*, III. I. 157.
resolve	*inform*, II. I. 86.
resolvde	*satisfied, convinced*, III. I. 38.
roundly	*fully*, IV. IV. 169; *promptly*, IV. IV. 231.
royall	*gold coin worth about ten shillings*, III. I. 131.
sack	*type of white wine from Spain and the Canaries*, I. II. 15 etc.
scabiosity	*the condition of having scabies (the itch)*, IV. V. 52.
secured	*over-confident*, II. II. 49.
seeld	*ceiled*, II. I. 323.
serjant, sergiant	*sheriff's officer, responsible for arresting debtors*, IV. III. 14 S.D., IV. V. 76.
setting forth	*equipping, adornment*, II. I. 262, III. I. 46.
sfoote	*(by) God's foot*, IV. V. 83.
shuters	*suitors*, III. I. 97.
slid	*(by) God's lid*, I. III. 72.
sli(e)ght	*cunning trick*, I. II. 25, III. I. 241.
slip	*omit*, IV. I. 5; *let slip, lose*, IV. IV. 256.
smack, smerck	*kiss*, II. I. 295, V. II. 61, 63.
sore	a sore fox: *very much a fox, a proper fox*, V. II. 58.
sowne	*swoon, daze*, II. I. 113.
standing cup	*cup with a foot or feet*, II. I. 344, 345.
standing wages	*fixed wages*, III. I. 136.
start	*flinch*, V. II. 169.

state	*estate, fortune,* II. II. 45, 76, III. I. 112; *outward display, ceremony,* I. I. 75, I. II. 27, IV. IV. 10.
sticke	*hesitate,* II. I. 168, IV. II. 11.
still	*always,* I. I. 11, V. II. 103.
stranger	*somebody not a relative,* I. III. 27, II. I. 367.
sure	*betrothed,* III. I. 24; *safe,* IV. I. 20.
take	*go to for refuge,* III. III. 119.
tast	*sample,* IV. V. 21; *take (the air),* V. II. 35
tearme	*period when the law-courts were in session,* III. I. 99.
tee	*thee,* II. I. 331.
teirs	*tierce, cask of wine,* V. II. 2, 3; *tears,* V. II. 3.
tell	*count,* II. I. 341, IV. IV. 233.
then	*than,* I. II. 49 etc.
this	*this is,* IV. V. 157.
thrists	*thirsts for, longs for,* III. III. 108.
tother	*the other,* III. I. 176 etc.; *other,* II. I. 277, IV. V. 148.
touch	*test,* II. I. 237, IV. I. 56.
toye	*trifle,* IV. II. 45.
trampler	*one who tramps about, intermediary, lawyer,* I. IV. 10 etc.
trasht	*bustled, ran busily,* I. IV. 60.
trayne, traine	*lure, entice,* III. I. 238, IV. II. 75.
tro	*trow you? do you think?* II. I. 161.
unmand	*without servants, without male escort,* I. II. 27.
unready	*undressed,* III. IV. 32.
valiant	*worth, good for,* I. I. 61.
vild	*vile,* IV. IV. 158.
vintner	*inn-keeper selling wine,* III. III. 68 S.D. etc.; *wine-merchant,* IV. V. 50.
wagtayle	*profligate woman, harlot,* II. I. 77.
wast-thrift	*spendthrift,* I. III. 26, II. I. 3.
watchet	*light blue,* IV. IV. 28.
whoreson	*fellow, chap (vulgarly jocular),* I. I. 68.
with-all	*with,* I. III. 2.
wring	*wrest, force,* IV. V. 116; *squeeze (amorously),* V. II. 163.
writings	*legal documents,* I. IV. 3, II. I. 34.
yee	*yea,* IV. IV. 85, IV. V. 29.

APPENDIX

Spellings in *A Trick to Catch the Old One* and *A Game at Chess*

In the Note on the Text, I have put forward the view that Q1 of our play was set up from Middleton's own manuscript. This view is based on the high frequency in Q1 of spellings also found in the Trinity manuscript of *A Game at Chess*, which is in Middleton's own hand; I shall refer to this as G, and to Q1 of *A Trick to Catch the Old One* as T.

G dates from about twenty years later than T. However, P. B. Murray[1] has shown that there is a good correlation between the forms used in G and those used in Middleton plays printed early in the century, irrespective of the printer, and that there is no such correlation between G and a number of plays by other authors; so it looks as though Middleton's spelling-habits did not undergo any fundamental change in the interim. Some of the evidence for the resemblances between G and T is already available in Murray's article: from his material, it is clear that they use the same weak forms and contractions, and the same forms of the verbs *have* and *do*: forms like *e'm*, *on't*, *ha's*, *'tis*. A comparison of G and T, however, suggests that Murray may have exaggerated the closeness with which Elde's compositors followed their copy. In fact the correlation between G and T varies for different items. Some of the variation can be explained by the demands of line-justification, especially as T is mainly prose; but Middletonian and non-Middletonian variants can often be seen side by side in T in cases where justification cannot be the explanation. In such cases it is to be presumed that the compositor used his own spelling instead of that of the copy, and it looks as though his resistance varied from item to item: for some forms he tended to follow his copy, his own spellings slipping in only occasionally; in others he regularly changed the forms in his copy, and Middleton's spellings show through only rarely. This can be illustrated by two extreme cases. (1) In G, final *l* is invariably doubled after a short vowel

---

[1] "The Authorship of *The Revenger's Tragedy*", in *PBSA* 56 (1962), pp. 195–218. See also G. R. Price, "The Authorship and the Bibliography of *The Revenger's Tragedy*, in *The Library*, 5th series, vol. 15, pp. 262–77.

(*vestall*, *evill*, *will*, etc.); in T it is doubled in 92% of the cases (451 out of 490), which is a pretty good correspondence. (2) G frequently uses initial *u* instead of *v*, and not only when it is vocalic (*uppon*), but also when it is consonantal (*uertue*, *uanish't*, etc.); this initial consonantal *u* is particularly common in the word *uerie* ("very"). But this is a spelling that compositors are extremely unlikely to reproduce, because it was a firmly established convention that only *v* should be used initially and only *u* medially. However, just one example has slipped through into the text of T: the word *uery* (III. 1. 233). The selection of examples that follows ranges between these extremes.

In G, the ligature æ occurs 30 times, in 19 different words; in more than half the cases it is in the prefix *præ-*; in T it occurs 5 times— *præcontract* (twice), *præiudice*, *præsum'd*, *præsumption*. G uses the spellings *ay* and *oy* in preference to *ai* and *oi*, even in non-final position (where they occur in nearly 98% of the cases); in T the figures for non-final position are *oy* 81%, *ay* 24%. G regularly uses the spelling *nck* (*drinck*, *ranckle*, etc.), except in *thinke* and *thankes*; T has 14 examples of *nck*, and 13 of *nk* (of which 8 occur in *thinke* or *thanke*). G uses *ei* in a number of words, including *peice*, *codpeice*, *beleife*, *cheife*, and *mischeife*: these spellings are all found in T. In a number of words G favours initial *en-*: *enuite* (2), *entend* (2), *encrease*, *enteruiew*, *encline*, but *intent* (2); T has *enuite* (4) beside *inuite* (2), *entend* (3), *enterchangeably*, but *intent* (1). In G the ending *-ness* is almost invariably *-nes* (62 examples) but occasionally *-nesse* (5 examples); in T, *-nes* occurs 10 times, and *-nesse* 24. G often uses *ti* instead of *ci*, e.g. *spetiall*, *antient*, *delitious*, *pretious*, *malitiouslie*; the five forms quoted all appear in T. G uses the forms *bee*, *hee*, *mee*, *shee*, *thee*, *wee*, *yee*; T regularly uses *yee* (twice only) and *thee*, but for the others it fluctuates between *be* and *bee*, etc.; the percentages of *ee* forms are *bee* 46%, *hee* 42%, *mee* 31%, *shee* 46%, and *wee* 43%. G has 25 examples (16 different words) of the use of *ʒ* where *s* was either normal or at least common; T has 18 such examples (11 different words); examples (found in both plays) are *riʒe*, *suffiʒes*, *cooʒen*. For final unstressed *-y*, G normally has *-ie*, though *-ye* appears occasionally; in T, on the other hand, the normal form is *-y*; however, *-ie* does occur in just over 10% of the cases, and *-ye* occurs once.

Some examples of spellings of single words: "Again": G *agen* (normal), *agayn* (1); T *agen* (23), *againe* (2). "Blood": G *bloud* (normal); T *bloud* (5), *blood* (1). "Close": G *closse* (3); T *closse* (3), *close* (2). "Devil": G *deuill* (11); T *deuill* (10), *deuil* (1), *deuile* (1), *diuil* (1), *diuuill* (1). "Enough": G *ynough* (normal), *enow* (1); T *inough* (9), *ynough* (6), *enow* (2). "Friend": G *frend* (7); T *friend* (18), *frend* (1). "Guests": G *guesse* (1); T *guesse* (2), *guestes* (1). "Hear": G *heare* (3); T *heare* (23), *here* (3). "Hour": G *hower* (3); T *hower* (10), *houre* (4). "Little": G *litle* (normal), *little* (1); T *little* (9), *litle* (7). "Master": G *M^r* (normal), *master* (1); T *maister* (normal), *master* (3). "Never" (contracted): G *nere* (4), *ne're* (2); T *nere* (24), *neere* (4). "Old": G *ould* (normal); T *ould* (4), *old* (1). "Plague": G *plauge* (2); T *plauge* (1), *plague* (1). "Strength": G *strenght* (normal); T *strenght* (1). "Strict": G *strickt* (3); T *strickt* (1). "There is" (contracted): G *there's* (normal), *theres* (5); T *there's* (20), *ther's* (6), *theres* (5). "Women": G *weomen* (6); T *women* (3), *weomen* (1). "Young": G *yong* (3); T *yong* (10), *young* (4).

Although there is no space to give the analysis, it can also be said that, in the past tense and past participles of regular weak verbs, there is a complicated pattern for the distribution of various endings (*-ed, -de, -d, -'d, -t, -te, -'st*), which is very similar in the two plays; particularly distinctive is the use of *-'st* after a *c* which is pronounced /s/, as in *disgrac'st, forc'st*.

It may be added that the light style of punctuation in T closely resembles that in G; and that, as one would expect, many of the Middletonian forms disappear from the reprint of 1616.

THE FOUNTAINWELL DRAMA TEXTS

Other titles available in the series:

Francis Beaumont: *The Knight of the Burning Pestle*;
ed. Andrew Gurr

Thomas Dekker: *The Shoemakers' Holiday*,
ed. P. C. Davies

George Farquhar: *The Beaux Stratagem*,
ed. A. Norman Jeffares

Ben Jonson: *The Alchemist*,
ed. S. Musgrove

Ben Jonson: *Volpone*,
ed. J. L. Halio

Thomas Kyd: *The Spanish Tragedy*,
ed. T. W. Ross

John Marston: *The Dutch Courtesan*,
ed. Peter Davison